EDITORIAL
"CHAN THE MAN"
By Rick Baker

Welcome to the latest issue of "Chan the Man," a magazine dedicated to celebrating the legendary Jackie Chan and his incredible contributions to the world of entertainment. We are thrilled to present an extraordinary collection of articles and features that delve deep into the life, achievements, and enduring charm of this iconic figure.

First and foremost, I would like to express my heartfelt gratitude to Darren Wheeling, whose exceptional cover design and article, "The Lost Interview," sets the tone for this remarkable edition. Darren's meticulous work captures the essence of Jackie Chan's enigmatic persona, and his article offers unique insights into an elusive interview that was long thought to be lost. Thank you, Darren, for your dedication and exceptional contribution. I would also like to extend my appreciation to Thorsten Boose, whose article, "The History of Jackie Chan with Horses," explores the fascinating relationship between Jackie and these magnificent animals. Building on the success of "Ride On," Thorsten delves into the profound impact horses have had on Jackie's life and career. It's a captivating journey that sheds light on a lesser-known aspect of Jackie Chan's multifaceted talent. Another crucial aspect of Jackie's cinematic magic is his voice. In "The Art of Dubbing: How Jackie's Voice Was Brought to Life," Paul Dre offers a comprehensive exploration of the man behind the dubbing, revealing the skill and dedication required to breathe life into Jackie's iconic voice. Thank you, Paul, for shedding light on this integral part of Jackie's cinematic legacy.

Also to Paul Bramhall's article, "Jackie Chan and Staley Tong: Giving the People What They Want," delves into the unique and enduring partnership between Jackie and his long-time collaborator, Staley Tong. Their combined efforts have consistently brought joy to millions of fans worldwide, and Paul's article pays homage to their remarkable synergy. Thank you, Paul, for celebrating their invaluable contributions.

I would also like to acknowledge the exceptional articles submitted by Simon Pritchard, Mike Nesbitt, and Mary Margaret McGoldrick, who have showcased their deep appreciation for Jackie Chan's work through their insightful contributions. Your articles add depth and diversity to this collector's item, making it a true treasure for any Jackie Chan fan.

Jackie Chan has entertained us for over five decades, and his enduring legacy is a testament to his unmatched talent and charisma. We hope this edition brings you joy, nostalgia, and a renewed appreciation for the man who continues to captivate us all.

Keep the faith

Rick

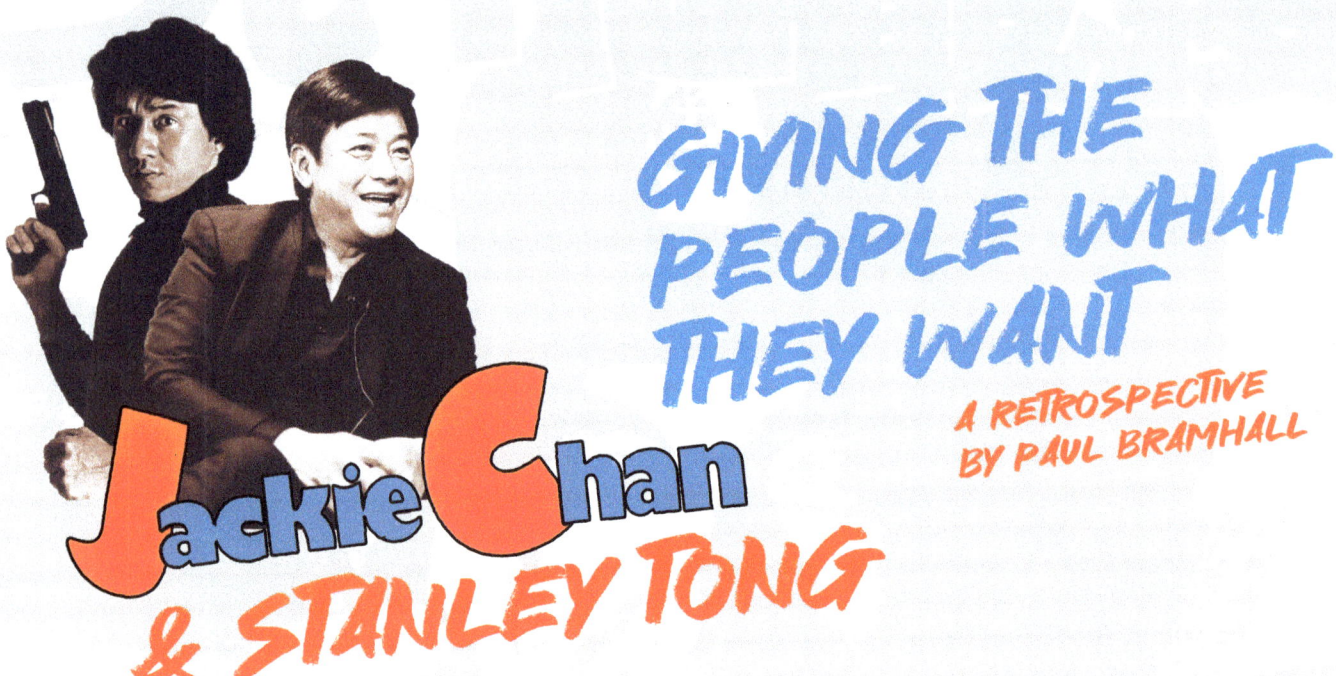

Giving the People What They Want

Jackie Chan & Stanley Tong

A retrospective by Paul Bramhall

It may come as a surprise, but the only director who's worked with Jackie Chan more than Stanley Tong is Lo Wei, and if the latest news about a sequel to The Myth is true, by 2024 the 2 directors will be neck and neck when it comes to working with one of Asia's most enduring action icons. Of course the relationship between star and director is quite different. Chan cranked out 7 movies with Lo Wei at the helm in the 4 years spanning 1976 to 1979, starting with the intolerable New Fist of Fury and concluding with Dragon Fist, one of Chan's best old-schoolers. It's well known that Chan wasn't happy being under contract to the Lo Wei Motion Picture Co., which is the complete opposite to the stars' relationship with Stanley Tong.

To date the pair have worked in the capacity of star and director 6 times, however unlike Chan's 4-year stint with Lo Wei, his collaborations with Tong have spanned a whopping 28 years. Sometimes leaving gaps of more than a decade between collaborations, the question of what keeps drawing Chan and Tong back together no matter how much time passes is an interesting one. With this feature, we decided to delve into their shared filmography to explore the theory that, whenever Chan wanted to produce a piece of sure-fire populist entertainment, Tong was the director he'd turn to.

Former stuntman Tong pulled a Jackie Chan-esque style move with his directorial debut in 1991, Stone Age Warriors, wearing multiple hats including producing, writing, choreographing, and of course directing. He stopped short of appearing in front of camera, but his can-do attitude was enough to capture the attention of both Chan and the execs at Golden Harvest, and within the year he was hired to helm the 3rd instalment in Chan's Police Story series. After spending the latter half of the 80's directing, starring, writing, producing, and choreographing most of his movies, in 1991 Chan would step into the director's chair for Armour of God II – Operation Condor,

after which he wouldn't direct again for over 20 years. Most likely exhausted, Chan was looking for someone else to do the heavy lifting behind the camera, and it was Tong who'd be offered the golden chance.

While many site Dragon Lord as being the production that saw Chan step away from traditional kung-fu and focus on a more stunt heavy action aesthetic, it would be Police Story 3: Supercop 10 years later which really saw that line of thinking come to fruition. In reality Chan still littered his movies after Dragon Lord with plenty of fight scenes, shifting from the traditional kung-fu style to modern kickboxing, with

productions that focused purely on stunt work (Project A II) being the exception rather than the rule. However Police Story 3 was different, not only being more stunt focused, but also marking the beginning of an era when the opposite came to pass. Post 1992 Chan's output noticeably shifted away from extended fights, making any movie that was fight heavy the exception (Drunken Master II, Who Am I?), and the stunt filled spectacle the new normal.

It's often said that Chan decided to move away from intricate fight choreography to focus more on spectacle heavy stunt work during this period in order to appeal more to an international audience, a possible pre-emptive move to break into Hollywood before the 1997 handover. While there's some merit to this theory, I'd argue its equally the case that Tong as a director was more interested in constructing stunts than he was choreographing or filming fight scenes. A look at his other titles as director, such as Project S and China Strike Force, show a similar approach that leans more towards extended action sequences rather than setting up fight scenes.

Regardless of Chan's international ambitions though, out of all his collaborations with Tong, it's 1992's Police Story 3 that feels most like a Hong Kong movie. All of their joint ventures involve globe-trotting in some way, and the third instalment is no different, taking place in Mainland China (which was treated like another country back in the early 90's!) and Malaysia. Here it feels like Chan is just about still playing Chan Ka-Kui, although the character is diluted of the intensity he came with in the first 2 entries, and his long-suffering girlfriend May, played by Maggie Cheung, is reduced to a throwaway cameo role. For all intents and purposes, Police Story 3's connection to the previous entries feels tenuous, with Tong's disregard for continuity showing up in instances such as Mars now cast as a villainous henchman rather than one of Chan's colleagues.

Future collaborations would dilute the line further between Chan the family entertainer and Chan playing an actual character, with storylines becoming increasingly simplistic and uninspiring, however in the Hong Kong cut of Police Story 3 there's at least some grit still on display. We witness girls being shot up with heroine, and one who's overdosed being disposed of in a particularly callous way, reminding us that the previous Police Story entries were never supposed to be kid flicks.

Tong's real ace up the sleeve helming his first big blockbuster though was the casting of Michelle Yeoh, here returning to the screen following her divorce from Dickson Poon of D&B Films, which saw her retired for 5 years. It was the first time for Chan to share co-star status with someone other than his Peking Opera brothers Sammo Hung and Yuen Biao, and such was his ego we'd have to wait 6 years for him to share co-star status with someone again, finally conceding to Chris Tucker for Rush Hour in 1998. When it came to sharing co-star status again with a woman it took a whole ten years, eventually succumbing to Jennifer Love Hewitt in 2002's The Tuxedo, a movie I'm not sure anyone would be willing to say was worth the wait.

Chan and Yeoh seemed to be looking to outdo each other in the action stakes, leading to a finale full of vehicular mayhem which includes highlights such as Yeoh jumping a motorbike onto the top of a moving train, and Chan hanging off a rope ladder attached to a helicopter high above Kuala Lumpur. So impressive is the final reel, that the fact Tong cast Yuen Wah and

Page 3

did precisely nothing with him is almost forgivable. Police Story 3: Supercop proved to be a success, leading to Tong not only being hired to helm Chan's attempt at breaking into the US a couple of years later in the form of Rumble in the Bronx, but also to create a spin-off movie for Michelle Yeoh's character. *Project S* (or *Supercop 2* as it's known in some territories) was released in 1993 and features an amusing cameo from Chan in drag as his character Chan Ka-Kui, which is almost worth the price of admission.

Chan had a tumultuous time in the intervening couple of years, banging heads with Wong Jing on 1993's *City Hunter* (which famously led Jing to cast Jacky Cheung as a satirical take on Chan's persona in 1995's High Risk), and replacing the preferred choice of Jet Li in Kirk Wong's *Crime Story* the same year. Chan's sheer ego led to more clashes in 1994, this time with the legendary Lau Kar Leung on *Drunken Master II*, whose creative vision was so different that he ultimately left the production before filming was complete. Needless to say that by the time 1995 came around, Chan was likely relieved to be working with Tong once more on their sophomore collaboration, a production intended to break Chan into the US market after several failed attempts throughout the early to mid-80's.

Rumble in the Bronx was in fact filmed in Vancouver, a fact given away by the occasional glimpses of the Rockies in the background. More so than *Police Story 3*, Chan and Tong's sophomore pairing would cement the type of wholesome action flick aimed at an international audience that they'd continue to crank out for the rest of the 90's. Playing a cop who ends up protecting a supermarket being run by Anita Mui (reunited after the previous years *Drunken Master II* where Mui played Chan's mother!) from a biker gang, *Rumble in the Bronx* shows all of the strengths of Chan and Tong's pairing, as well as all of its weaknesses. It was also the movie that famously coined the phrase – 'No Fear. No Stuntman. No Equal'. At least one part of that certainly wasn't true, however it was a tagline that Chan was more than happy to play to in the media.

What's perhaps most interesting about the 'No Stuntman' part is that the most impressive stunt in *Rumble in the Bronx*

isn't in fact performed by Chan, but rather by Tong stepping in as his stunt double. The stunt sees Tong jump off the top of a carpark building and land on a stamp sized balcony across the street to escape the biker gang, and is one of those heart jump into your mouth moments that only the most brazen of stunts are capable of inducing. Fight action is again dialled back, although ironically the brief bursts we do get deserve a mention in any discussion on Chan's choreography style.

Unlike the Wing Chun dummy action which is only teased in Wheels on Meals, more than 10 years on here Chan fully lets loose on the iconic apparatus in a suitably impressive display of power and precision. Similarly, when it comes to incorporating props into a fight scene, the sequence that takes place in the biker gangs' den is a masterclass in physical dexterity and sheer creativity. In a filmography filled with iconic prop usage, this scene is one of if not the best out of all of them. Everything around the action though is painful, with a questionable attempt at a plot that seems to have had less attention paid to it than some of those Hong Kong movies that didn't even have a script when they started filming. Chan is less a character here and more an onscreen personification of the all-round nice guy image that he increasingly fell back on in the 90's.

Apart from helping out a wayward Francoise Yip to get her life back on track, he also takes time to bond with her wheelchair bound kid brother (complete with English dialogue like "I wish my legs were normal so that I could play with my sister in the park"), played with a grating level of annoyance by Morgan Lam in his one and only film appearance. At its most incomprehensible, Chan ends up randomly making friends with the biker gang after he helps them to see their error of their ways (via offering to have a cup of tea together), which leads to a diamond smuggling group of gangsters being introduced into the plot from nowhere.

The lore behind Rumble in the Bronx is of particular interest, as it's well known that Chan broke his right ankle when he jumped onto the hovercraft in the bombastic finale. While it's frequently said that the injury prevented Chan from having a final fight scene that was planned, Tong's style of filmmaking makes for a legitimate argument that the whole hovercraft sequence was always going to be the intended finale. Adding to this line of thinking is a similar sequence involving a dump truck that would be used for the finale of Mr. Nice Guy, a production helmed by Sammo Hung a couple of years later that opted for a similar approach over any kind of final fight. Regardless of the mixed feelings towards the finale, Tong's approach had the desired result, and in 1996 Rumble in the Bronx was released across 2000 cinemas in the US making Chan a household name.

On top of breaking Chan into the US market, *Rumble in the Bronx* was also the top grossing Hong Kong movie for 1995, which pretty much guaranteed a Tong and Chan reunion. Audiences wouldn't have to wait long, as the following year they paired up once more for *Police Story 4: First Strike*, a production that was originally intended to be a stand-alone tale, but due to popular demand was rejigged to be another Police Story entry. How much effort went into rejigging it is debatable. *First Strike* is guilty of being the movie which kicked off the naming convention of whatever character Chan was playing being called, wait for it – Jackie Chan. Gone is the character known as Chan Ka-Kui, and instead Chan spends the whole moving answering to his own name. In many ways the cycle was complete, Chan was now playing himself.

Also gone was the intensity and sense of injustice that Chan imbued Ka-Kui with in his self-directed original and sequel, and in his place was the bumbling everyman who had a gift for fighting that came to dominate Chan's mid to late 90's output (see also *Who Am I?*). Even Maggie Cheung's long-suffering May is nowhere to be seen, replaced by a pair of novelty Koala bear briefs, with the only slim connection to previous entries being the presence of the late Bill Tung. What can't be denied is that First Strike cemented the Chan and Tong style of filmmaking – Jackie Chan plays himself in paper thin plots full of foreign 'actors' who behave like they belong in a kid's TV show, played off against showstopper stunt work. Out of all their collaborations it's this one which most embodies these elements, with its enthusiasm to appeal internationally often woefully misplaced.

Playing out like Tong's go big or go home homage to James Bond, *First Strike* ups the ante so much that Chan is now responsible for tracking down a stolen nuclear warhead that could blow America off the map (who said Chan only stopped being loyal to Hong Kong in the 2000's!?). Recruited by the CIA, here Vancouver is swapped for the Gold Coast in Australia, which notably isn't masquerading as any city it blatantly isn't. Like *Rumble in the Bronx* the primary language in First Strike is English, although there's also a variety of other languages spoken as well, of which the ridiculously broad Bogan-esque Australian tones certainly deserve their own mention. Speaking of Australia, this is a land down under where hotel rooms come with their own koala, surely setting up anyone who planned a vacation there after the movie's release for severe disappointment.

Tong is clearly enjoying playing with a large budget here (at least by Hong Kong standards), but it's also clear at this point that he doesn't have much ability as a filmmaker, with the characterisation and storylines if anything getting progressively worse after Police Story 3: Supercop. What First Strike shows Tong does do well is to construct a constant stream of action beats which prevent the audience from considering an early exit, and similar to the gang den scene in Rumble in the Bronx, here the pair also throw in a standout fight scene. The ladder fight in First Strike, which has Chan fending off several attackers by brandishing a foot ladder, shows all of the choreographic touches that make Chan's brand of action so entertaining, and is a triumph in creativity.

Equally entertaining but far less discussed is the hotel escape from 2 oversized burly bruisers (one of which is Nathan Jones making his movie debut), a sequence that perfectly balances physical comedy with high-risk stunt work performed so casually it almost risks not registering. Another trope that *First Strike* introduced is Chan's habit of 'introducing' his female co-stars. With no recognisable Hong Kong names like Michelle Yeoh and Anita Mui to rival Chan's screen presence, *First Strike* offered up the debut of Annie Wu, who spends most of the runtime either in or taking off a wetsuit (this 'introducing' trend would continue with Miki Lee the following year in *Mr. Nice Guy*, and Michelle Ferre in Who Am I? the year after). It's safe to say there was little risk of Chan being overshadowed by any of the female cast members anymore.

Like *Rumble in the Bronx*, *First Strike* was successfully distributed in the US, although it came with a whopping 20 minutes cut off its original 110-minute runtime. It was rumoured at the time that a fifth entry in the Police Story series was on the way, but the 1997 handover saw a mass exodus of Hong Kong talent leap across the pond to try their hand in Hollywood, and Chan and Tong were no exception. Their globe-trotting partnership that was anchored in Hong Kong didn't continue stateside though. Tong swapped out Chan for Leslie Nielsen (not a line I ever thought I'd write) to direct 1997's *Mr. Magoo*, and Chan hooked up with Money Talks director Brett Ratner for *Rush Hour*, which paired him with Ratner's Money Talks lead Chris Tucker.

Unlike Tong though, who after his Hollywood outing returned to Hong Kong (making China Strike Force in 2000), Chan would remain primarily working in the States for the next 6 years, intermittently popping up in HK movies for a cameo (with the exception of 1999's *Gorgeous* and 2001's *The Accidental Spy*). While many understandably figured Chan was enjoying being paid far larger amounts than he was in Hong Kong for doing far less (which gradually became truer the longer he was there), from interviews at the time of *Rush Hour's* release it seemed that he was genuinely frustrated at how risk-averse Hollywood was. Now needing to satisfy insurance safety standards and unions, even so much as jumping onto a container was considered a risky move, and Chan's distinctive action aesthetic found itself stifled and drowned out by his shouty co-star.

By the mid-2000's it seemed many of the fears of how much control China would exert over Hong Kong (and its film industry) were largely unfounded, and gradually the talent that had left HK began to come back. Chan was one of them, who returned to Hong Kong filmmaking in earnest in 2004 to headline director Benny Chan's *New Police Story*. Far from being the fifth entry that was rumoured after First Strike, this Police Story was a new tale with Chan playing a different character (to clarify – neither Chan Ka-Kui or Jackie Chan). Now 50 years old, Chan's more mature casting as a cop who becomes a depressed alcoholic after his team is killed off by a ruthless gang was largely seen at the time as a sign of things to come. That trail of thought didn't last long though.

By 2005 almost a decade had passed since Chan and Tong had worked together. In that time Chan headlined 12 movies (7 of which were Hollywood flicks), while Tong had directed, well, the previously mentioned China Strike Force. It's perhaps telling of Tong's directorial talents that he was all but out of work without his go-to leading man (or rather, being his leading man's go-to director), and even more so of just how much control Chan likely had over the productions Tong was directing in terms of creative input. Regardless of Tong's barren filmography though since they parted ways, after *New Police Story* Chan would team up with him once more for 2005's *The Myth*, which gave us the first Jackie Chan 2-for-1 since Twin Dragons.

Clearly looking to appeal to as broader audience as possible, *The Myth* aimed to tick a number of audience demographics, as all of Chan and Tong's productions increasingly did. Of course there was the loyal Hong Kong fanbase, who at this point had yet to sour to Chan (Willie Chen was still keeping him reigned in!), the increasing popularity of Korean cinema saw the casting of Kim Hee-seon (*Ghost in Love*) and Choi Min-soo (*Sword in the Moon*), and it was partially filmed in India with Bollywood bombshell Mallika Sherawat. Perhaps in one of the final examples of a Hong Kong movie catering to its Korean audience, the theme song Endless Love was sung as a duet by Chan and Hee-seon, with Chan singing in Mandarin and Hee-seon in Korean. Bring your barf bag.

The lead up to the release of *The Myth* was an entertaining one. Chan and Tong made a point in interviews of stating it was going to be a different type of Chan flick than audiences were used to seeing, and at its most absurd they called a special press conference in India to address rumours that were circulating around the casting of Mallika Sherawat. The rumour involved Sherawat's casting over other Bollywood actresses being down to her willingness to perform a scene which involved nudity. It got so out of hand that the press conference was called so that Chan and Tong could explain that Sherawat's casting was based on her acting talent and that alone (just like CNN reporter Michelle Ferre in Who Am I?!). Needless to say, those going into The Myth expecting the 'different type of Chan flick' to be one that involves nudity will walk away disappointed.

The Myth is both different and the same, coming across like 2 separate movies which have been uncomfortably tied together. Perhaps Tong should have called Godfrey Ho for some tips. In the Qin Dynasty era Chan plays a General tasked with delivering the emperor's bride-to-be, played by Hee-seon. Ambushed on the way, Chan and Hee-seon are the only survivors, leaving them to complete the journey alone and for a forbidden romance to flourish. In the present, Jackie Chan is Jackie Chan (I mean, archaeologist Jack). Chan heads off to India to investigate a claim involving rocks that can make stuff float, and while

raiding a tomb comes across a painting of Hee-seon, triggering memories from his past life as the Qin Dynasty General! Past and present collide in awkward and not entirely coherent ways, leading to a Chan and Tong flick which is different, but not necessarily better.

While the present-day narrative that takes place in Hong Kong and India plays out like a typical Chan and Tong collaboration, the Qin Dynasty era sections are tonally jarring, and show Tong as a director completely out of his depth. Throwing in a bombastically swelling orchestral score in practically every scene Chan and Hee-seon share together, it's cringe worthy stuff, which is a shame because

Chan's performance here is effective. He comes across as genuinely conflicted and increasingly exhausted by the weight of his own armour, a far cry from the familiar nature of the present-day scenes. The Myth's period battlefield setting predated Red Cliff by 3 years, which triggered a slew of similar period-set productions, with Chan himself returning a decade later in 2015's Dragon Blade, so here it was both fresh and truly 'different' to see Chan in such a setting.

However Tong's direction isn't strong enough to take advantage of the unique premise, so any gravitas Chan's performance earns is quickly dispelled by his superpowered horse (anyone who's seen The Myth will understand). The first Chan and Tong collaboration to incorporate (ropey) CGI, at one point Chan himself is rendered by CGI for the kind of jump he'd likely have made himself in the previous decade, heralding the first time for his fanbase to be confronted with the fact he was no longer in his life-risking prime. If anything, The Myth makes a 180 pivot from the stunt heavy focus of their 90's collaborations, and shifts to place more emphasis on Hollywood style special effects.

Like the biker gangs den sequence in Rumble in the Bronx and ladder fight in First Strike, The Myth still manages to give us one vintage Chan sequence, with a joyously creative conveyor belt fight set in a glue factory involving Chan and Sherawat taking on various attackers being a highlight. However the finale foregoes both stunt work and fight action for an SFX heavy sequence that has everyone floating around in an emperor's tomb. As a finale it marked the biggest departure to date of what audiences expected from a Jackie Chan flick, with Tong seemingly relying on the CGI environment filled with various floating objects to provide the spectacle over any kind of physicality. It was a strange ending to a strange movie, complete with a bloated 2+ hour runtime that at times felt much longer, proving that Chan and Tong were perhaps at their best sticking to what they know.

The Myth failed to kick start a new string of collaborations between Chan and Tong, and the pair wouldn't work together again for the next 12 years. Instead Chan chose to re-team with New Police Story director Benny Chan for Rob-B-Hood the following year, and would reunite a 3rd time for 2011's Shaolin. However the cinematic landscape that Chan played in was rapidly changing. While he resumed working in Hollywood for the latter half of the 00's, cranking out the likes of Rush Hour 3 and The Spy Next Door (as well as lending his voice to the Kung Fu Panda flicks), China's rapid economic development saw the rise of a burgeoning middle class that loved to go to the cinema. During the beginning of the 2010's cinemas were being built across China in their hundreds, quickly making the Mainland one of the biggest box office draws for movies to play to.

This global shift to where movies could make the most money saw an increasing number of US and China co-productions, which included 2008's The Forbidden Kingdom and 2010's The Karate Kid, but it was 2011 that proved to be a landmark year. 1911 marked Chan's 100th movie, and concurrently was made to celebrate the 100th anniversary of the founding of the Republic of China. While now China's jingoistic and propaganda heavy output is a given, 10 years ago productions like 2009's The Founding of a Republic (which Chan also featured in) and 2011's Beginning of the Great Revival where seen as overlong oddities aimed purely at a domestic audience. Chan's decision to headline 1911 as his landmark 100th movie sent a clear (and for many hard to swallow) message that he aligned himself with the Chinese Communist Party.

Much of his HK fanbase felt betrayed. Watching Chan crank out lacklustre Hollywood efforts was one thing, but positioning himself politically within the context of his role as a movie star felt like a knife in the back. Despite this, he still appeared to feel a sense of loyalty to his Hong Kong fanbase (even if it wasn't reciprocated), so before embarking on what looked set to be a more serious acting career focused on Mainland audiences, he decided to go out with a bang. In 2012 he'd step into the directors' chair for the first (and so far last) time since 1991's Armour of God II - Operation Condor, to direct a sequel to it no less, that would become

CZ12. Chan made it clear that it would be his last big action movie, citing the fact he was tired and felt the world was becoming too violent. He still intended to make movies, but after this his focus would be more on acting than fighting.

However the movie studios had other ideas. Almost 60, the following year he'd re-team with Little Big Soldier director Ding Sheng for *Police Story 2013*, a tie-in to the franchise by name only that once again saw Chan willing to play an age-appropriate role. However conflicts behind the scenes were reported in the press – Chan felt his role shouldn't involve any action at all, but the producers had slapped the *Police Story* tag on the title and insisted it needed Chan to fight at least once to appease audience expectations. In the end it felt like he didn't have much choice but to go ahead with the awkwardly shoehorned in fight scene that rightfully split audiences down the middle. Perhaps the lesson Chan took away from *Police Story 2013* was that, whether he liked it or not, studios wanted Mainland targeted action flicks based on when he was in his 40's, not his 60's.

So began a string of movies that were built around Chan attempting to re-capture his younger glory days for a new audience. 2016's Skiptrace saw him partnered with Johnny Knoxville in a collaboration which recalled his late 90's/early 00's Hollywood vehicles, and Railroad Tigers from the same year brought back a level of Tong-esque goofiness. It's perhaps not surprising then, that a year later we'd get our first Chan and Tong collaboration since 2005's *The Myth*. In 2017 the world was graced with *Kung Fu Yoga*, an apparent sequel to *The Myth* in much the same way that *First Strike* is a sequel to *Police Story 3: Supercop*. Chan is still the archaeologist character (now frequently referred to as "the greatest archaeologist in China"), and the selling point here is another jaunt across to India, however that's where the similarities end.

Kung Fu Yoga is arguably the most blatant

example of a propaganda blockbuster to come out of China in recent years, coming across as a barely concealed fluff piece to boost relations between China and India. Like Chan and Tong's collaborations in the 90's aimed at breaking into the US, here once more English is the primary language used, with Disha Patani in the Bollywood bombshell role that Mallika Sherawat played in The Myth. Ironically Chan, now 63, here seems to be playing a younger character than he was 12 years earlier. Watching him ogle Patani, 38 years his junior, is not something anyone really needs to see (and to think there were those who complained about the 22-year age gap between Chan and Shu Qi in 1999's Gorgeous!). However watching Chan eye up someone young enough to be his daughter is the least of Kung Fu Yoga's issues.

The many interactions between the Chinese and Indian cast, full of amicable smiles and banterous dialogue, are enough to make your ears bleed. There's a treasure buried somewhere along the China and India border, and it would be great if everyone teamed up to look for it together, not just because their partnership will help improve the relationship between the two countries, but it also algins with China's 'One Belt, One Road' initiative! This exchange actually takes place, with the only consolation today being that the 'One Belt, One Road' initiative is more than likely on ice, after Chinese soldiers stoned and bludgeoned 20 Indian soldiers to death in 2020 at the same border being discussed in the movie. Whoever said propaganda works?

When watching Kung Fu Yoga, in retrospect the dialogue in the likes of Rumble in the Bronx and First Strike is Oscar worthy, as are the action sequences. After Railroad Tigers this was the 2nd movie to partner Chan up with younger co-stars, here represented by K-pop boyband member Lay Zhang, "the most beautiful Chinese yoga coach" Miya Muqi, and one-time Bruce Lee actor Aarif Rahman. Not that any of them get to do much, with a surprising lack of any kung-fu or yoga. Instead, the runtime is filled with various escapades that involve our super friendly cast running away from CGI wolves, CGI hyenas, CGI snakes, and even a CGI lion that ends up involved in a car chase, which results in it throwing up CGI vomit. Apparently Tong didn't realise the error of his ways with the finale of The Myth, and if anything seemed to believe that audiences wanted more of it!

The barely there plot involves the families descendent who the treasure used to belong to hunting down Chan and co. to claim back what he believes is rightfully his, although Chan's impassioned yelling of "This treasure belongs to the Chinese government!" may make you feel differently. Played by Bollywood actor Sonu Sood, events eventually culminate in an underground temple in India (much the same way as The Myth finished up in an emperor's tomb, proving that Tong's 12-year hiatus obviously wasn't a breeding ground for new ideas). The scene gives an opportunity for Chan to throw some moves during a climatic face off against Sood, but Tong seems to be pulling his old "why can't everyone just get along?" philosophy here, originally displayed by Chan and the biker gang's reconciliation in Rumble in the Bronx.

There's no randomly shoehorned in gangsters here though, instead, the fight just stops mid-way through when Sood suddenly realises the error of his ways, which results in the whole cast (including Chan and Sood) breaking out into a Bollywood dance number. Tong even foregoes the trademark Chan outtakes over the end credits, instead choosing to extend the Bollywood dancing into a full-blown music video shot across multiple locations. The result of an aged star wanting to recapture his glory days for a new audience, an already average director out of practice by over a decade, and a government keen to push their agenda through the language of cinema, Kung Fu Yoga is horrible. I still recall watching it at the time of its release and feeling a sudden fondness for Chan and Tong's 90's collaborations, as their reunion here turned out to be a depressing low point for both of them.

In the aftermath of Kung Fu Yoga it was to be expected that Tong would go back into hibernation, probably hoping that Chan may give him a call in another 12 years (the thought of Chan still headlining action movies at 75 doesn't seem as far-fetched now as it did just a few years ago). As it happened though, Tong's luck was in, and he'd only have to wait 3 years to receive that call. In 2020 Chan and Tong reunited for their 6th collaboration in the form of Vanguard. As expected, Tong didn't do anything in the intervening 3 years, however Chan found himself as busy as ever. He returned to Australia to star in the Mainland sci-fi blockbuster Bleeding Steel (which is almost as bad as Kung Fu Yoga), headlined the CGI car crash The

Knight of Shadows: Between Yin and Yang, and clocked in a barely there cameo in the jingoistic epic *The Climbers*.

Interestingly, as if to give fans a cruel tease of the more serious roles he said he'd start taking on while promoting *CZ12*, in 2017 Chan also starred in *The Foreigner*, a brooding thriller from director Martin Campbell set in the UK. Playing a father after those responsible for a terrorist bombing in London that leaves his daughter dead, Chan is a revelation here. World weary and grizzled, the onscreen charisma that arguably helped carry those 90's collaborations with Tong is here transferred to a very different type of character, resulting in Chan's best movie in almost 20 years. Despite only being made 6 years ago at the time of writing, *The Foreigner* is clearly an anomaly in his recent filmography, and as entertaining as it is, it's also torturous to know this is the type of movie Chan could have been making if he'd followed through on his aspirations.

The Chinese Communist Party ramped up its influence in the film industry even more after the release of *Kung Fu Yoga*, with the board which approves film productions for screening transferred to sit directly under the department responsible for propaganda creation. With Chan firmly established as a bankable star in the Mainland, *Vanguard* very much feels like a Chinese Communist Party sponsored blockbuster. Whereas *Kung Fu Yoga* was all about promoting China and India relations, here we're reminded of China's dubious infrastructure investments in Africa, portrayed onscreen of course as being a wonderful friendship between country and continent. Except that, similar to Wu Jing's *Wolf Warrior 2*, in Vanguard Africa is also bizarrely referred to as if it's a country. A country with a brave Chinese girl on a mission to protect the African wildlife no less.

"So brave", as one character says without a hint of irony, but alas the girl is the daughter of a Chinese businessman whose former partner was involved in a terrorist group called the Brotherhood of Vengeance. The partner was killed by US forces, and now his son wants to take revenge by getting his hands on a weapon of mass destruction, so it's up to Chan and his highly patriotic and courageous security company to protect both father and daughter, plus make sure the US

doesn't suffer any casualties. Playing the CEO of the 'Vanguards', Chan's acting here is his poorest to date. He seems to want to play his CEO role seriously, but stripped of a director like Martin Campbell or Kirk Wong to bring out the nuances in his performance, instead of bringing a sense of gravitas to the role he just looks rather listless.

Vanguard is also the first of the Chan and Tong collaborations to feature Chan speaking predominantly in Mandarin, ditching the Cantonese and English of their previous movies. Despite his more age-appropriate role here as the CEO, Chan ultimately ends up getting in on the action just as much as he did in Kung Fu Yoga, without so much as a logical explanation as to why he decides to join his young co-stars on their mission to Africa. The co-stars in question this time around see Tong and Chan reunite with Miya Muqi, who's joined by Mainland actors Yang Yang and Ai Lun (whose character at one point is gifted a Captain China badge from his son, who proudly states he's "mightier than Captain America!", which give some idea as to *Vanguard's* level of subtlety).

Arguably more than any of their previous collaborations, here Tong crams *Vanguard* with action, the main issue is that it's completely uninspiring. Compared to his droll faced chants of "We will be victorious!", Chan seems to break character whenever he's called on to fight, which suddenly see him become a comedic buffoon complete with the 'shaky hands' gag being used twice in the same scene. The main action beats here though involve gratuitous amounts of gunfire. Whatever reservations Chan had in 2012 about the world becoming too violent it's safe to say have been cast aside, as we witness him gunning down plenty of faceless terrorists in a climatic shootout that spills onto the streets.

The biggest problem with *Vanguard* though is an overreliance on CGI. If I was a betting man I would have said after *Kung Fu Yoga* I doubt we'd be seeing any CGI animals turn up in a Jackie Chan movie again. Thankfully I'm not, since *Vanguard* sees the return of both CGI hyena's and another CGI lion (minus the vomit this time). The biggest problem though is the way CGI is incorporated into the big set pieces, and is essentially used for any of the showstopper

moments that once would have been done for real. There's a chase scene involving jet-ski's (in a sequence that saw Chan almost drown when he got trapped under a rock after coming off one), however when the jet-ski launches itself off a rock, or does a harrowing turn on the edge of a waterfall, it's CGI. We also get gold cars chasing each other, but whenever one of them crashes or goes airborne, it's CGI.

Tong used to be able to compensate for his directorial failings with his strength as an action director, which was further compensated by a charismatic action star. Stripped of both, with action that's been created by technology rather than practical effects, and a star who looks bored for most of the runtime, and what you're left with feels brash, noisy, and overwhelmingly empty. If Kung Fu Yoga was a fluff piece for China and India relations, then Vanguard is about China's image maintenance in Africa, and more 'One Belt, More Road' promotion in the form of a lot of mutual back patting between Chan and the Dubai police (at one point Chan realizes his Dubai counterpart understands Mandarin, to which his counterpart explains it's because his wife is Chinese, and Chan replies, "Oh, your wife is Chinese, she must be beautiful!" in a scene which is played completely straight.)

Since the release of Vanguard Chan and Tong have wound down their output considerably, no doubt confounded by the COVID-19 pandemic that saw China under severe restrictions that started in 2020, and only eased up towards the end of 2022. Amazingly, it was during this period that Tong would direct his first non-Jackie Chan starring production since 2000's *China Strike Force* in the form of *Rising Shaolin: The Protector*, a passion project for its star Wang Baoqiang which went straight to iQiyi and VOD in 2021. It also marked the first time for Tong to go straight into production on another movie after his last since his 90's heyday, and needless to say if you thought he was a weak director before, this won't be the movie to change your mind.

Chan himself would only clock in a cameo for the Hong Kong film industry benefit flick All U Need is Love from the same year, however with brighter times ahead and cinemas starting to come back to life, it would be in 2023 that the pair would once more find each other. For the first time sharing the screen with Chan in a movie where he isn't at the helm, Tong appears alongside Chan in Larry Yang's nostalgia fuelled *Ride On*, which sees Chan playing an aging stuntman in a surprisingly effective sentimental meta-journey down memory lane. Not surprisingly, their appearance fully leans into the meta-aspect of the narrative, with the pair appearing in a scene involving a film set (no spoilers for those who have yet to check it out), and it's admittedly hard not to smile at the sight of them together in such surroundings.

Perhaps their onscreen reunion is what led to the decision to once more reunite in the roles of star and director, as soon after the release of Ride On it was announced that a sequel to The Myth would be going into production, which as of the time of writing is titled A Legend. Does that make it a trilogy if we include Kung Fu Yoga, or does it put to rest the theory that Chan's Indian themed adventure should be seen as a sequel to The Myth after all? Regardless, so far all we know is that Chan is back as an expert archaeologist, and when he notices that the texture on some artifacts that were discovered in a glacier are the same as on a jade pendant he's been dreaming of, he sets off on an adventure to find the truth. One thing is for sure, we can probably expect more CGI animal shenanigans, and perhaps some flying around as well.

A Legend will be Chan and Tong's 7th production as star and director, having worked on and off with each other for over 30 years, and seemingly no limit in terms of how much time passes before they work together again. What can't be denied is that Tong has helped Chan breakout into whatever market the star had his eye on at the time – from the US with the likes of Rumble in the Bronx and First Strike, to re-establishing himself with Hong Kong and pan-Asian audiences with The Myth, through to solidifying his Mainland appeal with Kung Fu Yoga and Vanguard. Together they gave the people what they want, even if those people weren't always us, and for that their partnership is admirable. Whatever audience A Legend turns out to be targeted at, chances are Chan and Tong will deliver exactly what that audience wants. They always do.

GIDDYUP!
A RIDE THROUGH JACKIE CHAN'S FILMOGRAPHY
By Thorsten Boose

A German- proverb says "The greatest happiness on earth, lies on the back of the horses". Although this popular saying can be traced back to ancient Arabic wisdom, the core of the statement seems to be universal. Horses enjoy a high status in human history – as they do in film culture around the globe.

Film stories about real and fictional horses abound: Black Beauty, Fury, Jolly Jumper, Seabiscuit, Mr. Ed and, if you want to, the Last Unicorn. We only know their origins from Western pop culture. In 2023, however, director Larry Yang and actor Jackie Chan surprise us with their Chinese film "*RIDE ON*". In the actual leading role: the film horse Chitu (赤兔) as the stunt horse Red Hare. Even though it was announced early on that Plaion Pictures will be responsible for distributing the new Chan vehicle in German-speaking countries, my fellow countrymen and I still have to be patient until it is released. Other countries such as China, Thailand, Russia, the UK and Canada are among the lucky ones who have already been able to watch this very special Jackie Chan film.

When life gives you tomatoes
In the meantime, many professional critics have scrutinised the film, and Jackie Chan fans worldwide are almost unanimous: "RIDE ON" touches the heart. The Rotten Tomatoes platform, however, only awards the film 57 % on its Tomatometer, whereas the audience seems to be enthusiastic about the film and is pleading for a whopping 81 % satisfaction. The numbers can still change, of course, but it already seems from countless reports on social media from all over the world to be a successful, if somewhat different Chan film that combines classic comedy, a little action and a lot of emotion.

I would be interested in Senh Duong's personal opinion at this point. The film portal Rotten Tomatoes was actually founded because of Jackie Chan. Senh Duong, Patrick Y. Lee and Stephen Wang were three students at Berkeley University in California, USA, in 1998. The project was spearheaded by Senh Duong's enthusiasm for Jackie Chan films and "*RUSH HOUR*", which was announced for August at the time. Duong was so excited by the film's marketing that he began collecting reviews and critics and posting them online. In just two weeks he had built and published the website, but then the release of "RUSH HOUR" was postponed until September. To pass the time, he integrated other films into his database and gradually the Rotten Tomatoes site we know today was born. Even though according to RT critics "RIDE ON" is considered rotten with 57 %, many of the critics say that two elements stand out positively: the passion for stunt work and the actual main character Chitu, the horse.

Those who have not yet seen the film (like me), but have studied some video clips, BTS, and interviews may have realised that Jackie Chan has established an intimate relationship with his four-legged co-star. And this is exactly what has been a challenge for Chan, as he originally suffered from a fear of horses, equinophobia.

Director of the film Larry Yang put it this way in his own words in an interview about the film: "Among us filmmakers, they say the hardest thing on a film set is working with kids and animals." And yet, on the set of "*RIDE ON*", Chitu got a lot of love from the team and, most importantly, professional care from trainers and grooms. Out of hundreds of horses cast, Chitu prevailed for the role alongside Jackie Chan and, according to Larry Yang in the interview, will retire as a star.

In the tradition of horses.

So how does Jackie Chan, born in Hong Kong, relate to horses? First of all, it is interesting to know that according to the Chinese horoscope he was born in the Year of the Horse, 1954. In Chinese tradition, the horse stands for freedom, and in Mongolia it is still revered today. People born under the sign of the Horse are said to have a lot of energy – sometimes a little too much. For these people, chasing their own dreams is the drive in life, money and success are secondary.

Men born under the sign of the Horse are said to have a strong independence and a selfless willingness to help others. But sometimes they overestimate themselves – that will become interesting in the course of this text. The year in which Jackie Chan celebrated his breakthrough in Hong Kong was also a year of the Horse, 1978. The image of the tortured Jackie Chan in the Horse Stance (Ma Bu) is still world-famous today.

But first let's jump 23 years into the past to get to the bottom of Jackie's fear of horses. On 24 May 2000, a 46-year-old Jackie Chan sat with Jay Leno and gave an interview about his new film "*SHANGHAI NOON*" (2000). Those who remember those days look back with a smile at Jackie's statement at the time that he would soon stop making action films.

In the finest Chon Wang manner, cowboy Jackie Chan rides into the studio at the beginning of his performance on a real horse in front of a live audience. A childhood dream must have come true for him to have conquered Hollywood not by storm but on horseback. Even as a child, Jackie Chan loved his cowboy costume. He is sitting next to Halle Berry, which I personally find very interesting, because both were "immortalised" by the same artist in 1997 and 1998 respectively. Joseph Malara reports in his book "Celebrity Sculptures & Hands of Stone, My Story" about how he made hand and face prints of the stars Jackie Chan and Halle Berry; both before their respective breakthroughs in Hollywood: Jackie Chan with "*RUSH HOUR*" (1998) and Halle Berry with "*X-MEN*" (2000).

After his ride, Jackie is approached by talk show host Jay Leno about a big problem.
Leno: "You once told me that you were afraid of horses."
Chan: "Yes, when I was on a film set very early on, we young stuntmen were asked who could all ride a horse. They all raised their arm, so I thought I'd better do that too. Because that meant double pay. Everyone but me was chosen for the scene, so I waited in frustration. The scene ended and all of a sudden all the horses came back

without stuntmen. My friends had all either broken their arm or their ankle. From then on, I never volunteered to ride again." Jackie doesn't reveal which film it was, but he goes on to say that his four-legged co-stars never listened to him when he had to work with one afterwards. Perhaps this was due to his lively, youthful energy, which still bubbles out of Jackie today at almost 70 years of age. Typical horse according to the Chinese horoscope. With Chitu, Chan has probably found his master.

For "*SHANGHAI NOON*" (2000) it was clear to the makers that Jackie Chan had to deal with horses not only theoretically but also emotionally. The star was given lessons in horsemanship and in return the four-legged friend had to follow Jackie everywhere with the help of trainer Claude Chausse. By the way, did you know that the scene in which the film horse Fido sits down in the film runs backwards? Horses can't sit down like dogs. When they stand up, however, it looks like that for a moment.

On 25 August 2000, BBC's Rebecca Thomas writes in "Chan's Hollywood horseplay": "With more than 100 films over 36 years under his belt - not to mention countless broken bones - Chan's commitment to his art is clear. But the 46-year-old had to overcome a fear of horses for Shanghai Noon. Jackie Chan Chan is proud that he conquered his fear of horses "Stunts like jumping from the train were easy but getting on the horse was scary - I've had some bad experiences with horses," he explains." Isn't that what makes a Jackie Chan film so special? The real Jackie Chan takes on a seemingly unsolvable task and overcomes fears and obstacles to present a result that not only entertains but also motivates. Already at the promotional time of "*SHANGHAI NOON*" (2000), a short review could have been made, a review of films in which Jackie Chan plays side by side with horses. Let's take a look at some of those appearances.

Of horses and horsepower

Jackie stated in countless interviews over the decades that he had worked on hundreds of films as a young stuntman, and indeed there are still a few appearances by him in wuxia and kung fu films being re-discovered now and then. One of them is "*THE BLACK TAVERN*" (1972). Although strictly speaking Jackie does not actually interact with a horse here, it is worth pointing out the fight together with his

later buddy and stunt team colleague Mars, which takes place in front of a horse that is tied to a carriage. You can see that the quadruped is visibly frightened when the fight breaks out – could have gone wrong. Jackie has made several appearances as a coachman in his career. Also in John Woo's "*THE HAND OF DEATH*" (1976), when he gives Dorian Tan a lift. In "*HALF A LOAF OF KUNG FU*" (1978) he has to trot along as a dolt next to a noble lady riding her horse. In the German dubbing there is an allusion that is appropriate in terms of content, which is unfortunately lost in English (they say donkey instead of fool):

James Tien: "Talking to him is like casting pearls before swine."
Jackie Chan: "I'm no swine. And you're no pearl. In fact, we're alike. We're just a couple of fools."

In the 1980s, the Eastern film thematically outgrew the Qing dynasty into modern

times, which of course meant fewer horses but more horsepower: The quadrupeds were replaced with fast-paced motorbike and car chases.

Nevertheless, Jackie Chan made it back in front of the camera with a horse in 1984 in a commercial for the fashion company Guy Laroche. At the beginning of the elegant watch commercial, he rides through the vastness of Australia until he catches sight of the beautiful Michelle Yeoh on a bicycle. Afterwards, the two meet again on other means of transport until the found couple breaks the fourth wall next to a horse at the end of the commercial. Now Oscar winner Michelle Yeoh was crowned Miss Malaysia in 1983 and appeared here alongside Jackie Chan in one of her first ever acting jobs. Also in the 1980s, Japanese photographer Sumio Uchiyama, or Uchi for short, often travelled alongside Jackie Chan to provide the latest snapshots for his home audience. In fact, Jackie often called him his favourite photographer back then. So, also in Australia around 1988, a photo set was created

JACKIE CHAN
PHOTO MEMORY

with Jackie and a horse. Fans can see a few prints of it in the book "Jackie Chan – Photo Memory" (published 01/1989 in Hong Kong).

Despite his fear of horses – which was certainly pushed a bit by the media (thanks, Willie!) – Jackie Chan also worked with the faithful four-legged friends in the 1990s. For example in "*MR. NICE GUY*" (1997). Here, TV chef Jackie inadvertently becomes a coachman as he tries to calm two rambunctious grey horses harnessed in front of a carriage. A classic Jackie Chan action-comedy scene that was not entirely without danger, shot in the streets of Melbourne.

Pride goes before a fall

In the 1990s, the triad situation in Hong Kong came to a head as many well-known actors, directors and producers took to the Hong Kong streets to demonstrate against the mafia's criminal activities and interference in the Hong Kong film and music landscape. When the storm was mostly over, the millennium was also coming to an end. And suddenly, a mentor of Jackie Chan, Golden Harvest co-founder Leonard Ho, passed away.

Leonard Ho was an avid fan of horse racing and like many of Hong Kong's wealthy businessmen, he was a member of the prestigious Hong Kong Jockey Club (HKJC) (香港賽馬會). Horse racing was brought to Hong Kong by the British as early as 1846, and those who wanted to be part of high society in modern Hong Kong of the 1990s met in the VIP boxes of the Happy Valley Racecourse (跑馬地馬場) on Hong Kong Island. Yuen Biao and Sammo Hung were also said to have been members of the Hong Kong Jockey Club, but Jackie remembered what his father had once forbidden him to do many years ago: no gambling! But now Jackie was an adult and after a thorough check to see if he had any unpaid bills with the triads that would damage the HKJC's reputation, he became a member of the Hong Kong Jockey Club in the late 1990s, living on the tradition of his mentor Leonard Ho. In the same year that Jackie Chan was a guest on Jay Leno, he bought a racehorse from New Zealand and named it Hong Kong Star (冠昌之星). It is rumoured to be a tribute to Leonard Ho. The New Zealand racehorse was in good hands and was prepared for upcoming races by trainer Peter Ho Leung throughout its career. Its first race was on 3 November 2001, the last on 7 May 2003. In its second race, Hong Kong Star had an exciting race with Nichsolas Tse's sire's horse, Game of Life (遊戲人生). But as in the first race, Jackie's four-legged friend failed to score. Instead, another horse named Myth (神話) is said to have inspired Jackie's later film of the same name. A few weeks later, Hong Kong Star improved slightly, but in its entire career, which spans only 14 races, the highest finish was third.

I have published all 14 races of Jackie Chan's HONG KONG STAR in a 42-minute video with official statistics of the HKJC on YouTube! Just scan the QR code or check my channel "Jackie Chan Deutschland".

In respected circles, there was indeed damage to the image of Jackie Chan, whose racehorse was ridiculed by professionals who had been investing, trading and generating revenue for decades. Even experts who had allegedly helped select Hong Kong Star for Jackie Chan were questioned about their professional abilities. Hong Kong Star

HONG KONG STAR
ALL 14 RACES IN HONG KONG
JACKIE CHAN'S RACEHORSE

the Horse 1978 became a hubris in another Year of the Horse 2002.

The Millennium Extravaganza was an official event to celebrate the advent of the New Millennium. It was held at the Happy Valley Race Course in the evening of December 31, 1999. On this picture we see Jackie Chan riding a horse during his entrance at 10.30 pm.

The man, the myth, the legend

The Hong Kong Jockey Club
RIDING HIGH TOGETHER

was ranked so low that people allegedly called for Jackie Chan's resignation from the Hong Kong Jockey Club behind closed doors. What exactly is true about all this and whether the failures were the fault of the horse, jockey or trainer is known only to those involved. However, if you don't know your way around a multi-million-dollar business like horse racing, you can sometimes get ripped off by buying a sick or not so motivated horse.

Hong Kong Star earned only 105,000 Hong Kong dollars in his career, which was divided among all employees. Saddened by the failure, Jackie Chan withdrew more and more from horse racing – Donnie Yen, Aaron Kwok and others, on the other hand, showed up more and more often at the racetrack from 2003 onwards. What was Jackie Chan's breakthrough in the Year of

But Jackie Chan wouldn't be Jackie Chan if he didn't let a failure get him out of character. After he retired from horse racing, more films followed in which he used horses, not only in "SHANGHAI KNIGHTS" (2003).

Even in his animated series "JACKIE CHAN ADVENTURES" (2000-2005), which contains many references to his films and Chinese culture, horses are thematised. After all, the horse talisman is one of the twelve talismans that are supposed to keep the evil Shendu in check. The strengths of the horse talisman: healing and regeneration. What a powerful symbolism for the man Jackie Chan himself, who for decades to this day has always managed to recover from setbacks and surprise his audience.

In "AROUND THE WORLD IN 80 DAYS" (2004), Jackie mounts an electro-mechanically driven carriage as Passepartout, in short a kind of automobile, and one could include this as an ironic reference in this list. But just a few cuts later, Jackie again

plays the coachman behind real horses. As explained above, legend has it (pun intended!) that it was during Hong Kong Star's second race on 21 November 2001 that the spark for "*THE MYTH*" (2005) ignited. A great anecdote if true, in any case Jackie shot a real blockbuster for his 2005 film with real and partly CGI horses, the sequel of which is currently being shot with director Stanley Tong. Whether the team in "*THE LEGEND*", which is to be seen from 2024, has learned from dealing with Chitu from "*RIDE ON*" (2023), in which Stanley Tong has a guest appearance, and will horses also be used in the new film? Let's wait and see.

Jackie Chan also swings back into the saddle in the fantasy epic "*FORBIDDEN KINGDOM*" (2008). In the same year he advertises with a horse for the Olympic Games in Beijing. And a few years later, dozens of four-legged extras are hired for "*DRAGON BLADE*" (2015). In many ways, 2023's "*RIDE ON*" sets a milestone in Jackie Chan's filmography. One of them is definitely the direct acting contact with an animal, which has never been seen before in Jackie Chan films.

On 4 April 2014, Jackie Chan opened the International Akhal-Teke Horse Association Conference & China Horse Culture Festival at the Imperial Ancestral Temple in Beijing as an ambassador for the Chinese Horse Festival. To coincide with the Year of the Horse, the theme for the conference was Peace, Heritage and Dream.

So we can be curious to see what impulses an almost 70-year-old Chan will draw from his experiences on the set of "*RIDE ON*" (2023). And indeed, he already announced in a video interview with Sina from April 2023 that he had further plans for films with animals:

"I'm going to make a film with Stanley Tong called "*I AM NOT A PANDA*". I also have an idea to shoot with a dog."

It seems that Jackie Chan has found a new challenge for his films, if action and stunts really don't work out at all anymore, animals could become a new element of a chantastic filmography.

Another sideline that seems to be coming back to the fore after years of neglect is dubbing work. Again, Jackie Chan lent his voice to some animals in the past, such as Master Monkey in the "*KUNG FU PANDA*" films or the Monkey King in "*MONKEY KING: HERO IS BACK*" (2015). In "*THE NUT JOB 2: NUTTY BY*

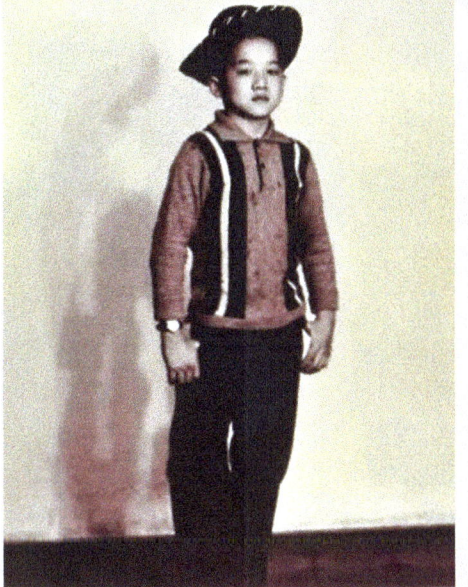

NATURE" (2017) he shouts the legendary words "Don't call me cute!" as Mr. Feng, the mouse.

"*BEAUTY AND THE BEAST*" (1991) and "*WISH DRAGON*" (2021) I mention for the sake of completeness, but am happy to point out Summer 2023 in closing. Here, English-speaking fans will hear Chan the Man for the first time as Splinter in Seth Rogen's new TMNT adaptation "*TEENAGE MUTANT NINJA TURTLES: MUTANT MAYHEM*". And perhaps from 2024 onwards he will continue as Master Monkey in the "*KUNG FU PANDA*" series. So far, no Jackie Chan dubbing jobs as a horse ...

FANATICAL DRAGON PRESENTS
5 FINGERS OF DISCS

Welcome once again Dear Friends, to this special issue dedicated to everyone's favourite little fortune, the one, the only Jackie Chan!

The bulk of my article this issue round, is actually dedicated to another of Jackie's classmates, the incredible Yuen Biao, in a piece originally penned for the Yuen Biao special, which didn't manage to get in there in time, but as there is considerable overlap in some titles (ie, they also feature JC) and things have been a little quieter on the JC Bluray front of late, its finding a happy home here in this issue.

Since I wrote the article originally though, there have been a few new developments and a couple of new announcements, so let's take a look at those first!

Gorgeous
88 Films
Region A+B Bluray.
Available Now

One of JC's movies that tends to divide opinion from fans, really as it's so unlike his other films from this era, and is in truth, really more of a vehicle for the spellbindingly stunning Shu Qi (sighs). It is very notable for a very different and much more bittersweet reason since the passing of the incomparable Brad Allen however, and is best remembered to me as being one of Brad's best on screen performances and one of his best on-screen hand to hand battles with Jackie.

Directed by regular Stephen Chow (who incidentally also cameos here) collaborator Vincent Kok, the film focuses on a young Taiwanese girl named Bu (played with zeal by Shu Qi) who after finding a romantic message in a bottle, heads for HK to find the man of her dreams, only to find out the author of the note, Albert (played by Tony Leung Chui-Wai) turns out to be Gay. All is not lost however as she meets a wealthy businessman named CN (Jackie Chan) and they fall for each other. If all of this sounds very much like it's going to be devoid of the usual Jackie Chan action hallmarks, you are not wrong! but there are still some action scenes as Jackie's character spars with his business rival Howie Lo (played by Emil Chau) and his goons, and its during one of these spats, that Howie brings in a higher from overseas to sort out CN, and that's where the wonderful Brad Allen comes into play.

The sequence that JC and Brad put together for the movie remains a high bar for both actors, as Brad, a long time member of JC's stunt team, really knows and works well with Jackie's timing and rhythm. It's worth tracking down this release for this and this alone, if the romantic subplot doesn't float your boat (or message in a bottle)

88 Films have put together a great release for the movie, porting over the rare Jackie Chan commentary track from the old Sony DVD release and adding in a heartfelt tribute to Brad from fellow JC stunt team member Andy Cheng as well as an archival making of featurette, interview with the director Vincent Kok and Two Brand new Audio commentary tracks, one by the wonderful HK based dynamic Duo themselves Mike Leader and Arne Venema as well as a a track by Frank Djeng joined by FJ Desanto.

Both the HK and International cuts of the movie are present here too with the old English dub being an option on the international cut, and Cantonese on both edits of the film, we also get a couple of music videos and the HK and English Trailers.

The stunning artwork on the slipcase (and bundled poster) is by Sean Longmore.
All in all a great release for a movie i still really enjoy, though maybe slightly more for the presence of the beautiful Shu Qi than anything else!

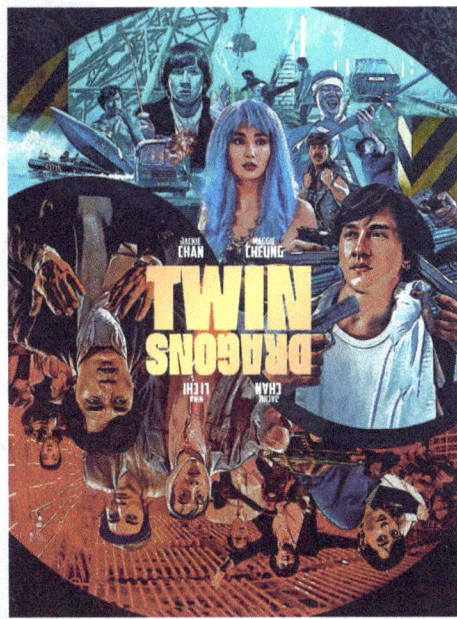

Twin Dragons
88 Fims Deluxe Bluray
Region B Bluray
ETD - July 2023

July of this year will see the release of one of JC's movies I've been most longing for on Bluray (and in its original HK cut) the excellent Twin Dragons!
Co-directed by Ringo Lam and Tsui Hark, the film often gets criticised for its root scoping work (Jackie plays two roles in the films, twin brothers, separated at birth) but 88 have revealed the artwork for a deluxe edition of the film, so expecting a pretty great package for the movie, which in its HK form has an absolute stack of cameos and some great supporting performances from Maggie Cheung, Chor Yuen and Nina Li Chi. Artwork is once more by Sean Longmore, special features details are still to be revealed, but you can look for a full review in a future issue.

New Fist of Fury
Arrow Video
Region A Bluray
ETD - August 2023

A very recent announcement just as we were going to print on this issue comes from Arrow Video, who have picked up the rights to one of the OG brucesploitation flicks
Lo Wei's 'official' sequel to Bruce Lee's Fist of Fury, the imaginatively titled..

New Fist of Fury. With Nora Miao returning to the character she played in the original, but this time relocating to Taiwan where she encounters Jackie Chan's Chen Zhen V2.0 aka
Ah Long.
This is a title many of us in the UK will already have a more than serviceable Bluray edition of thanks to 88 films, but Arrow have really managed to push the boat out in terms of new extras for the release, and it's being put out as a US only exclusive in August of this year

The confirmed extras are as follows:
• New 2k restoration from the original negatives by Fortune Star
• High Definition (1080p) Bluray transfers of the 120-min Original Theatrical Cut and the 82-min 1980 Re-release Cut
• Original Mandarin and English lossless mono audio for the Theatrical Cut, plus newly uncovered alternate Mandarin and Cantonese mono audio
• Original Cantonese and English lossless mono audio for the Re-Release Cut
• Newly translated optional English subtitles
• New feature commentary on the Theatrical Cut by martial arts cinema experts Frank Djeng & Michael Worth, co-producers of Enter the Clones of Bruce Lee
• New feature commentary on the Re-Release Cut by action cinema expert Brandon Bentley
• New Fist, Part Two Fist, a new video essay by Bentley comparing New Fist of Fury to the rival sequel made simultaneously, Fist of Fury Part Ii
• Trailer gallery, including a Chen Zhen trailer reel of sequels and reboots
• Image gallery
• Double-sided fold-out poster featuring original and newly commissioned artwork by Tony Stella
• Reversible sleeve featuring original and newly commissioned artwork by Tony Stella
• Illustrated collector's booklet featuring new writing by Jonathan Clements and an archival retrospective article by Brian Bankston

It's not a movie i would usually be tempted to double dip on, but the glorious artwork by Tony Stella, and the new Brandon Bentley commentary track as well as a second track by Frank Djeng and Michael Worth make this a pretty tempting proposition!

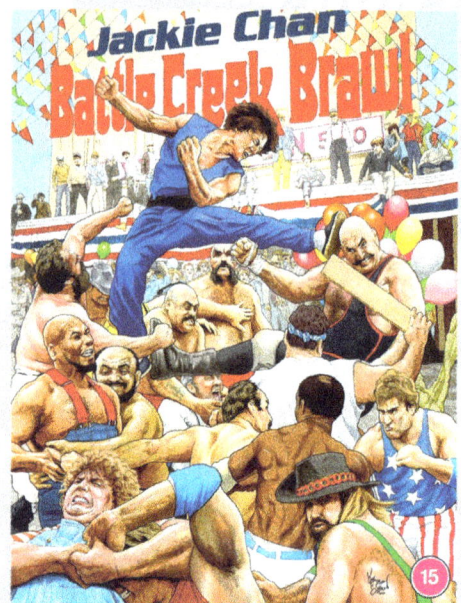

Battle Creek Brawl
88 Films Deluxe Bluray
Region B
ETD - Still to be confirmed.

Another tease this one, 88 films have released the all new artwork for an upcoming deluxe edition of Jackie's first big attempt to break the US market, his collaboration with Enter The Dragon director Robert Clause: Battle Creek Brawl. This was actually one of 88's first Jackie Chan Bluray releases, and the 88 boys clearly want to up the ante and give the movie the deluxe treatment overhaul. Artwork is by the Sharpie Samurai himself the wonderful Kung Fu Bob O'Brien but no release date or further info has been provided so far.
As soon as we know more, y'all will too.

Dragons Forever
4K / BR
Region A+B - 88 Films

88 films long awaited 4K / Bluray Deluxe Edition of the last great 'Three-Dragons-together-in-one-movie' movie…Dragon's Forever arrived in style in the UK late last year.
And in the USA in early January.
Previously 88 had released this twice in the UK as a regular Blu-ray, and then in a limited edition steelbook, but never before in the US.
The decision to release the movie again, but this time upgrade it to the 4K/UHD format and add in new extras, both printed and on disc, seemed like a no-brainer. In this past year of Yuen Biao treats, this felt very much like the definitive icing on the cake. It's a truly glorious release.
Dragon's Forever celebrates it's 35th anniversary this year. So the timing feels perfect to pull together all the best of the various Bluray and DVD releases that have come before, upgrade them to 4K and wrap them all up in super shiny new artwork by new 88
Uber talent, cover artist Sean Longmore. Add in an all new commentary track on disc by the busiest man on the Bluray commentary circuit, the master of remaster himself, Frank Djeng, here joined (as he was on Eureka's Police Story 4K Boxset) by FJ Desanto. The two play off each other well and FJ brings his own very entertaining experiences and memories of the movie industry to the table, making for a really amusing, informative and re-listenable track. We also get a new interview with the truly amazing Chin Kar-Lok.
On the printed side of things we get some glorious Repro lobby cards, a double sided poster and a hefty book all housed inside one of 88's now standard Deluxe rigid full slipcases. All the extras that were on 88's previous Bluray release have all been ported over too, giving you hours and hours of bonus content to work through as well as several different cuts of the movie, including the famed Cyclone Z Japanese cut.
This is quite possibly 88 Film's single best release to date. It's impeccable.

The Prodigal Son / Warriors Two
Region B Bluray - Eureka

This is one I've previously covered in the regular issue run of the magazine, but how could we not shoutout once again to what may well be Yuen Bio's 'best' Kung Fu performance, certainly, it's amongst his most beloved, and this double pack from Eureka delivers a truly jaw dropping remaster of the Golden Harvest classic, alongside another of Big Brother Sammo Hung's best Martial Arts movies of the time, Warriors Two. But this release is on the list for Prodigal Son, and this timeless ode to Wing Chun is well backed up by extra features on disc. We get: A Brand new feature length audio commentary by Asian film expert Frank Djeng (NY Asian Film Festival) joined here by martial artist / actor Robert "Bobby" Samuels alongside a second new commentary by the HK Boys, Mike Leeder & Arne Venema. Archival interviews with Sammo Hung, Yuen Biao, Frankie Chan and Guy Lai. Alternate English credits, A Stills galleries including rare production stills, artwork, and ephemera and Trailers. If you got in there early there was a O-Ring slipcase and booklet featuring artwork by Eureka regular collaborator and our cover artist here,
Darren Wheeling.

On The Run
Region B Deluxe Edition BR
88 Films

This one seemed to catch a fair few people off guard when it came out last year from 88 as another of their Deluxe Editions, being maybe a film less well known by the old Hong Kong Legends DVD crowd and the newer post Boutique Bluray label fans. This great Neo-Noir Thriller is most notable for showcasing Yuen Bio's acting skills far more than his already very well established action chops and 88 Films have put together a killer package for this 1988 classic. Alongside the brand new, stunning 2K restoration of the original negative we get newly remastered English subtitles.

An Audio Commentary with Kenneth Brorsson and Phil Gillon of the Podcast On Fire Network as well as a second Audio Commentary with Asian Cinema Experts Frank Djeng again joined by FJ DeSanto.
Running Away - A new Interview with Alfred Cheung
Predicting the Future - An Interview with David West
An Alternate Ending and Hong Kong Trailer
And then 88's usual impressive arsenal of printed extras now commonplace in their Deluxe sets. A Reversible sleeve with original Hong Kong poster artwork and new artwork created by the one, the only, the Sharpie Samurai, Kung Fu Bob O'Brien. who has delivered a neon soaked, vibrant slice of art for the cover, which looks even better on the included poster. 6 x repro Lobby cards and the bound book all wrapped up in one of their rigid full slip cases. It's a great package for a real gem of a movie, the well thought out extras only serve to expand ones appreciation for this often overlooked example of HK Noir.

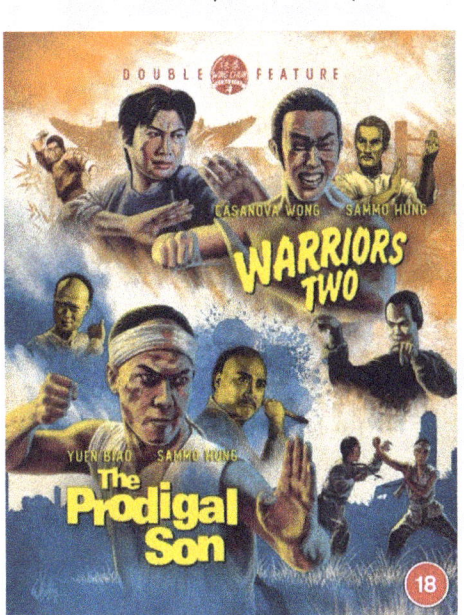

Dreadnaught
Region B BR - Eureka

Another from Eureka's continued journey through the Golden Harvest / Fortune Star back catalogues brings this absolute belter, Yuen Woo Ping's Dreadnaught, starring Yuen Biao alongside the OG Wong Fei Hung; Kwan Tak Hing, in an action packed Kung Fu Slasher film that was a real highlight for me amongst a sea of highlights last year from the label. The restoration on this movie is an absolute joy, especially in the darker scenes and in the detail in lead villain Yuen Shun-yee's Kiss inspired Make Up. The fight sequences in this are pure Yuen Woo Ping artistry. One spectacular 'fire cupping' scene in particular with the incomparable Kwan Tak Hing alone make this movie an absolute must own.

Extras wise we get Cantonese and English dubs, Optional English Subtitles, newly translated for this release, a brand new feature length audio commentary by Asian film expert Frank Djeng and a second brand new feature length audio commentary by action cinema experts Mike Leeder & Arne Venema along with an archival interview with actress Lily Li (21 mins) and Trailers

Zu Warriors of the Magic Mountain
Region B - BR - Eureka

It's easy to forget with this recent run of Yuen Biao centred movies, that Eureka had already put a couple out years ago, back before we really hit this new Golden Age

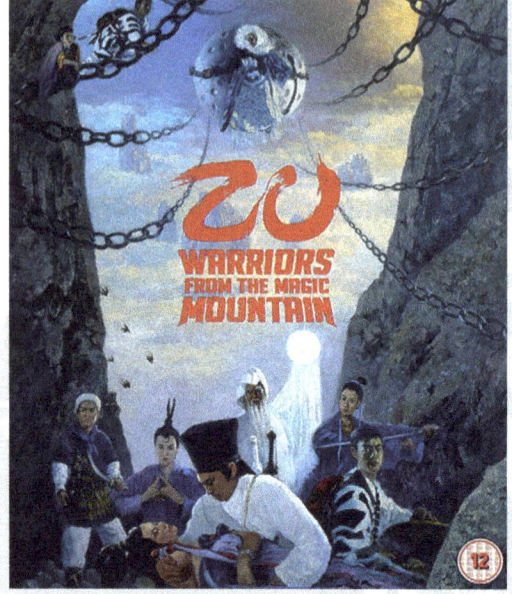

for HK releases, and before a legion of new fans joined in on this incredible period of high quality, beautifully restored versions of classic HK cinema coming onto Physical Media.

And one other such classic that Eureka already put out several years back, is Tsui Hark's seminal fantasy classic, Zu Warriors from the Magic Mountain. Yuen Biao and Sammy Hung star together alongside a host of other HK legends and a very young Moon Lee in this special effects laden spectacular that was seemingly the inspiration for John Carpenter's Big Trouble in Little China. Eureka have put together an impressive package of extras for the film, including a Brand new and exclusive select scene audio commentary by critic and Asian cinema expert Tony Rayns a Brand new and exclusive interview with Tsui Hark – a lengthy and in-depth interview with director Tsui Hark filmed in 2020 exclusively for this release.

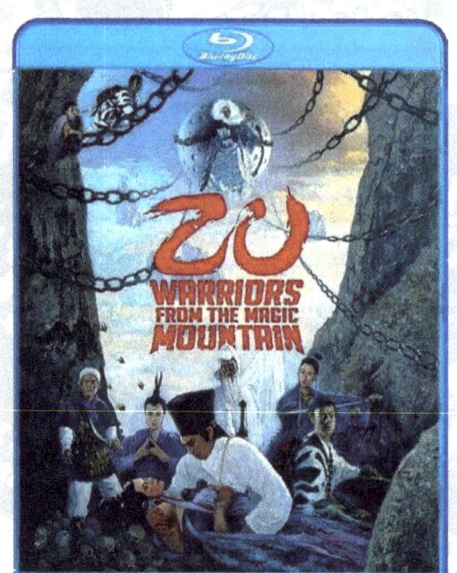

Zu: Time Warrior [93 mins] – the export cut of the film produced for European theatres, featuring a wraparound segment with Yuen Biao as a modern-day college student who is transported, Wizard of Oz style, to 10th Century China
Tsui Hark – episode of Son of the Incredibly Strange Film Show originally aired on British television in 1989 - this is worth the price of admission alone, these episodes were GOLD!
Alternate opening credits, restored to their original Western presentation
Archival Interviews with Yien Biao, Mang Hoi and Moon Lee and Trailers.

SHOUT SELECT - US VERSION

Now JUST as we were going to print with this issue, Shout Select released their own version of Zu over in the USA, it ports over almost all of the UK editions extras (apart from the Jonathan Ross TV show episode - boo!) but adds in a whole raft of new extras instead, i've not checked out the new disc yet, but it also includes:
A new Audio Commentary With Hong Kong Filmmaker And Academic Gilbert Po And Critic Sean Tierney
From West To East – A new interview with Visual Effects Consultant Peter Kuran
Riding A New Wave – Author and academic Victor Fan analyzes a Tsui Hark masterpiece
The Majesty and Magic of a Hong Kong Milestone – Academic Lin Feng looks back at an East Asian Action Classic

This actually bring us on to one of the (maybe predictable) knock on effects of this current Golden Age for HK Physical Media. Namely, the rise in regularity of two separate boutique labels both bringing the same title to market in the same time period, usually on different sides of the Atlantic, sometimes in collaboration, but increasingly, in a degree of healthy competition. This has led to inevitable label loyalties which in turn gave rise to a Blur Vs Oasis style label war going on in the various comments sections of facebook groups, forums and beyond with some fans vowing to stick by one label, others keen to double dip and some just left plain confused. But fear not Dear Reader, we've dived into the differing versions of each of following releases to let you know which comes out on top in the first ever Eastern Heroes…

Battle of the Biao's !!

DISCLAIMER -

this wee Biao Battle Royale is just for a bit of fun, and ALL the work being done both here in the UK by Eureka, 88 Films and Arrow Films , and in the USA by Vinegar Syndrome to restore, preserve and showcase the movies we love so much should be celebrated. The truth is whichever version of the following movies you go for, you won't be disappointed. Even for those with deep enough pockets to satiate a need to double dip, there is enough different here between a few of the releases to make that worthwhile and not enough difference whatsoever on a few others so hopefully this will help you decide which version will be the right fit for you!

ROUND ONE

Righting Wrongs
Region A Bluray (BR)
VS - Vinegar Syndrome

Righting Wrongs was a title many of us were waiting patiently for a decent release of,
for a long, long time. One of Yuen Biao's best leading man roles, playing a lawyer by day, vigilante by night who has to join forces with Cynthia Rothrock to go up against corrupt cop Melvin Wong. Some of the action sequences in this movie rank way up there amongst the best Yuen Biao ever put to film. It's an immensely satisfying action movie and one with multiple different endings, which I was rather curious how any potential special edition would handle..

First out the gate on releasing the movie was Vinegar Syndrome who brought out Cory Yuen's incredible action thriller in a 3 disc Special Edition boxset as a US or Region A title. The set offers Three different unaltered original feature-length presentations of the film, including: the original Hong Kong cut (96min) with Cantonese, English & Mandarin language tracks along with newly translated Cantonese-to-English subtitles; the extended and vastly different Mandarin language export cut (100min) with newly translated Mandarin-to-English subtitles; and the English friendly ABOVE THE LAW cut (92min). Most of the extras presented here are exclusive to VS's release, with a brand new commentary from Cynthia Rothrock along her archive track from the old laserdisc release. A third commentary track is also here from our men in HK big Mike Leader and Arne Venema backed up with brand new interviews with Cynthia Rothrock, Melvin Wong, Karen Shepherd and Peter Cunningham along with archive interviews with Yuen Biao, Cynthia Rothrock and Peter Cunningham, on disc extras are rounded out by a video essay by Samm Deighan and trailers for the movie and for the best of martial arts doc.

The other big selling point for VS's version is the inclusion of 'THE BEST OF MARTIAL ARTS FILMS (1990)" (91min) this feature-length documentary hosted by John Saxon includes footage and interviews with Cynthia Rothrock, Yuen Biao, Karen Sheperd, Jackie Chan, Kareem Abdul-Jabbar, Bruce Lee and many more!
This documentary is very much a fan favourite and had many folks excited to see it on here though since the set was released it's been confirmed that the documentary will be included in as yet unnamed UK release sometime this year and that in the UK release, all the clips in the doc would be properly formatted and remastered, which there are not in the version included on the VS disc.

Also included in the set is a 40-page perfect bound book with essays by film programmer Pearl Chan, author and martial arts historian Grady Hendrix and filmmaker/fan Simon Barrett * Artwork for the set is a mix of the original Thai poster art on the inside slipcase and newly commissioned cover art on the front and rear of the outer slipcase by the wonderful Tony Stella

Righting Wrongs
Region B Deluxe Edition Bluray
88 Films

Coming out a few months after Vinegar Syndrome's release and arriving in a far larger, deluxe sized package, came 88 Films Region B version of the movie released here in the UK and managed to up the ante with a new 'ending randomiser' feature which does exactly as it's name suggests and is a very cool feature indeed!
You have the option to watch any of the three cuts on their own, and multiple commentary tracks are provided across the different cuts, Frank Djeng on the HK cut, Cynthia Rothrock's original Tai Sent Laserdisc track as well as all new scene specific commentary tracks by Cynthia Rothrock and Peter Cunningham.
We also get Mike and Arne providing a track on the longer Singapore cut of the movie.
All the new tracks are excellent, Frank's track is loaded with his standard treasure trove of facts and insights. Mike and Arne's track brings the guys usual mix of HK tales, laughs and random thoughts.
We get new interviews with Cynthia Rothrock and Peter Cunningham and the same old archive interviews VS used with Rothrock and Cunningham.
Where 88 really push the boat out is in the printed extras, we get 6 x reproduction lobby cards, a mammoth 80 page bound book, a poster and a full slip case with gorgeous new artwork by the sublimely talented Sean Longmore.
All in all, 88 take the edge on packaging and presentation of the movie and the extra bits and pieces that go along with it,

the ending randomiser is pure Brandon Bentley Genius and something I hope we see used on more releases down the line.

WINNER - 88 Films!
The Brandon Bentley Ending Randomiser & Sean Longmore Art
One-Two punch gives 88 the win over VS, but it's damn close and tempered by the encouraging news that the great Best of Martial Arts Documentary will be coming to the UK soon.

ROUND TWO

The Iceman Cometh
Region A BR
Vinegar Syndrome

VS and 88 went toe to toe immediately after Righting Wrongs and both delivered special edition of The Iceman Cometh or 'The HK Highlander' as I often hear it being described, which does it a disservice, as its a great time travel comedy with some great action in places, but really this is the Maggie Cheung / Yuen Biao show for much of the movie, her taking advantage of his naive fish out of water time traveller brings most of the movies big laughs, and Yuen Was is on fine demented form as the villain. Clarence Fok directs the whole feature with a bombastic energy and style that makes the movie hold up pretty well.

Vinegar Syndrome's release again arrived first, sporting pretty great cover art by VS regular Robert Sammelin on the box and the slipcase and presenting a Studio supplied master with additional colour grading and restoration performed by VS We get the 115 minute 'Hong Kong Cut' presented in its Cantonese original language with newly translated English subtitles and two English dub soundtracks (original and a late-period redub) alongside an Alternate 122 minute 'Mandarin Export Cut' with it's original mono soundtrack with newly translated English subtitles. There is a brand new Commentary track with film historian & author Samm Deighan
A video extra, "Frame by Frame, Frame by Frame" - a brand new interview with cinematographer Poon Hang Sang, archive interviews with Yuen Bias and Yuen Wah along with trailers and a booklet with essay by John Charles.

The Iceman Cometh
Region B Deluxe Edition BR
88 Films

88 again followed up with their Deluxe equivalent here in the UK, and again offering the same two cuts as are on offer on the VS version, commentary duties on the 88 version come from two tracks, one from the busiest man working in Physical media, Frank Djeng and another track by the Podcast on Fire boys, Kenneth Brorsson and Phil Gillon. Both are first rate, and both are impeccably researched!
88 have also drafted in Arrow/Criterion Regular, the mighty Tony Rayns to record a video piece on The Iceman Cometh and on it's Director Clarence Fok. It's great to see Tony on an 88 release! Hopefully if 88 roll out more Shaw Brother's titles in 2023 we may see more of Mr Rayns involvement there too, fingers crossed!

Anyways, back to the Iceman Cometh, we also get a new interview with the Director, a David West video piece on the film and the old Hong Kong Legends DVD archive interviews with Yuen Bias and Yuen Wah which also graced the VS edition.
88 have found an old VFX before/after comparison reel which is fun, and again they absolutely excel when it comes to printed extras, which if you're a fan of premium editions, you will be a fan of these 88 editions. They hold up very well against the really, really high end boutique Bluray premium labels from the likes of Manta Lab, HDZeta etc. And they tend to offer far, far more on disc extras than those types of releases generally do, but the printed materials easily match the premiums for quality and quantity. We get another meaty

bound book, 6 x repro lobby cards, I ADORE these repro lobby cards, real lobby cards are a pain in the butt, they're usually weird sized, hard to store, pricey to frame and really, really expensive. Getting a more manageable sized set of cards that fit inside the box is a really great bonus. the poster is always cool to have and the fullslip cases are well built and beautifully printed, in this case, once more showcasing more art by Sean Longmore. All in all, in both the two first Vinegar Syndrome Vs 88 Films matchups, 88 Films present the more enticing package overall, and for those of us in the UK, far better value for money than importing the VS editions. But for my US friends, or for those of us multi region enabled, the Vinegar Syndrome editions are pretty much equally stunning and it's just very, very cool to see an independent US label bringing out more and more HK movies onto Bluray and 4K. We will see more and more examples of doubling up between the US and UK labels this year, with Burning Paradise already out from VS in the US and coming from Eureka in the UK soon, Ebola Syndrome available in 4K from VS in the States and now from 88 Films on blurry here in the UK. It can be hard to keep track of who is releasing what when and with what extras. This is a massive part of what i cover routinely over on my Youtube channel, so if you're keen to keep up to date with the latest release information and reviews. please jump online and check out my reviews and videos there..

WINNER - 88 Films - But again, both versions are pretty closely matched, just slightly different extras and packaging overall.

ROUND THREE

Wheels on Meals
Region A BR- Novamedia
VS
Region B BR - Eureka

Less to say about this one, it's a movie we all absolutely know and love and Eureka released a pretty great version of it a few years ago (though i wouldn't be too surprised if a 4K edition didn't show up at some point from somebody)
Nova Media in Korea had also released this a few years back with the same Fortune Star transfer as Eureka had used, but recently they gave it an overhaul and fancy new packaging with the original vintage HK poster (the super cool cartoon sketch one) It has most of the same extras, but on the Nova disc you don't get English subtitles for the extras. that artwork though. stunning.

WINNER - DRAW - Eureka on extras. Nova on Packaging.

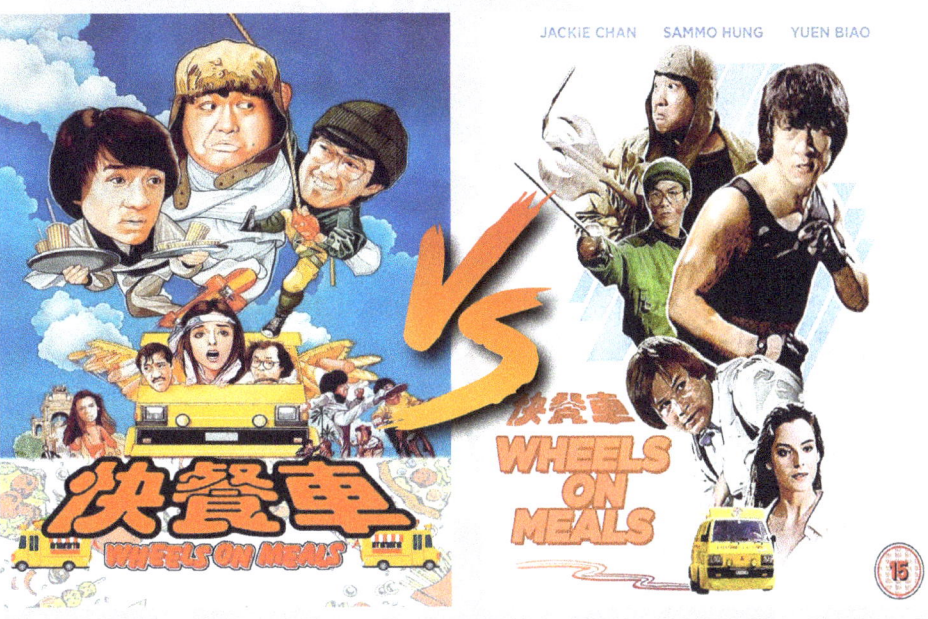

ROUND FOUR

Knockabout
Region A BR - Arrow Entertainment
Vs
Region B BR - Eureka

Recently Arrow Video and Eureka Entertainment have joined forces and partnered on a few releases, with the idea being that Eureka will bring the titles out in the UK and Arrow Films US will release the movies in the USA. This will allow them to share production costs and expand their respective lines further in each country. The first one of these titles was The One Armed Boxer last year, then this has been cemented by even more shared releases of Johnnie To's Running Out of Time, then the great Angela Mao set Hapkido / Lady Whirlwind and now this Sammo Hung classic, Knockabout.
For anyone with a multi region machine, for any of these releases from R.O.O.T onwards if you set the region to either US or UK you will see the menu screen change to the other label's logo and page..they are 100% the same disc, just different box art, disc art and booklet.

So Arrow now bring Knockabout to the US in all it's glory, looking absolutely spectacular and with a package of extras now standard for these Martial Arts releases from Eureka back in the UK, Two versions of the film presented in 1080p on Blu-ray from 2K restorations (Original HK Theatrical cut and the shorter Export Cut), The Original Cantonese mono audio, Optional English dubbed audio, Optional English Subtitles, newly translated for this release,
A Brand new feature length audio commentary by Asian film expert Frank Djeng (NY Asian Film Festival) a second brand new feature length audio

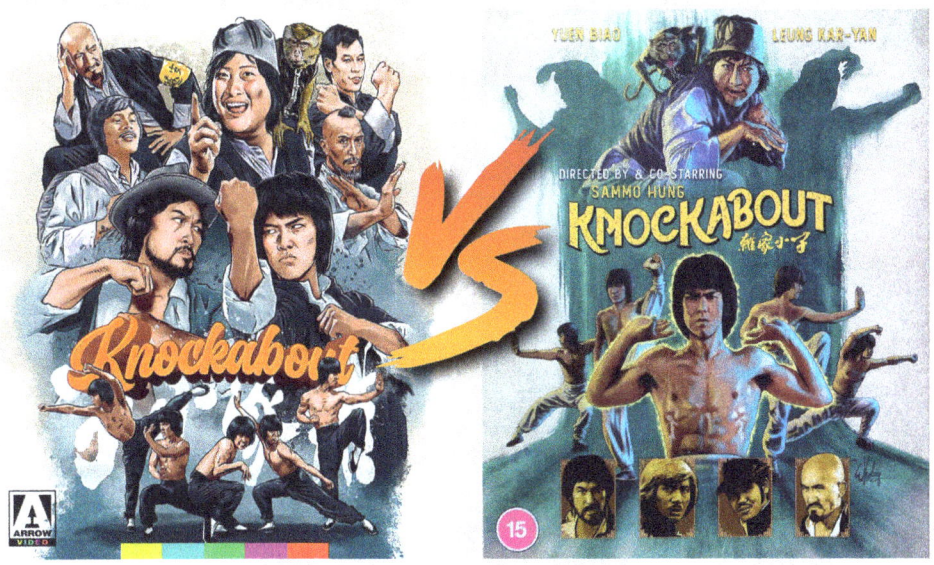

commentary by action cinema experts Mike Leeder & Arne Venema,
Archival interview with Sammo Hung,
Archival interview with Bryan "Beardy" Leung Kar-yan,
Archival interview with Grandmaster Chan Sau Chang (aka The Monkey King), a master of Monkey Style kung fu and Trailers.

If you got in early in the UK there was a slipcase featuring art by this issue's own wonderful cover artist Darren Wheeling. Our US friends were given a slipcase with cover art by the incredible Ilan Sheady aka Uncle Frank Productions… 'won't the real Llan Sheady please stand up, please stand up.

jokes aside, I'm a huge, huge fan of Llan's work. he also created Arrow's cover for their
One Armed Boxer release and has handled art duties on Arrow's version of the Angela Mao set too. For real deep dive Cover art fans, Llan has also worked quite often with German Mediabook masters Nameless Media and with the great Canadian label Raven Banner.

WINNER - DRAW - They're 100% Identical apart from the Cover Art, Booklet and Menu Screen

ROUND FIVE

Millionaires Express
Region A BR- Arrow Entertainment
VS
Region B BR- Eureka

One of the two all time classic, immense, epic Sammo Hung directed Yuen Biao starring movies, Eastern Condors gives us Sammo's War epic and this, Millionaires Express aka Shanghai Express, gives us his Western, albeit a Western fused with Eastern sensibilities and jam packed with more cameos from HK's finest than you can shake a stick at, or cram into one tiny wardrobe with…

Hold an old time western handgun to my head and ask me my all time favourite Sammo Hung movie, and chances are it'll be a three sides coin toss between this, Eastern Condors and Pedicab Driver.
But Millionaires would take the top spot more days than not. It's a powerhouse of a movie, a perfect blend of comedy, action, some truly jaw dropping stunts courtesy of Yuen Biao and Shaw Brother's veteran and

personal hero, Hsiao Ho. The only thing the movie is lacking is well, Jackie Chan, as his inclusion into this film would have pushed it through the stratosphere and would likely now have it being remembered as the ultimate Dragons movie.

But as it stands still, it's just a gem of a movie, now looking better than we ever imagined possible. Just about to be released in the US as we go to Print on this special issue will be Arrow Video's version of the incredible Millionaires Express release that Eureka gave the UK last year, this two disc set was absolutely loaded with extras including an all new Brandon Bentley supercut of the movie..In the UK the Two disc set sold out fast and is now since long out of print but this upcoming Arrow release in the US gives those that missed out on the Eureka edition a second chance to track it down, it's an immense release, one of the best standalone Martial Arts related titles Eureka have put out so far in terms of quality and quantity of extras and the Arrow version I'm sure will make that same mark in the USA when it comes out in March. The set contains HD presentations of the original Hong Kong Theatrical Cut and the Extended "International" Cut.
Original lossless Cantonese mono audio on both cuts, plus English mono audio for the Extended Cut, Newly created Optional English subtitles for both versions,
A brand new Commentary on the Theatrical Cut by Frank Djeng and a second new Commentary on the Extended Cut by Mike Leeder & Arne Venema Select scene commentary by star Cynthia Rothrock, moderated by Frank Djeng Three new video interviews with Cynthia Rothrock, A New Frontier and Express

Delivery - two archive interviews with Sammo Hung Way Out West, an archive interview with Yuen Biao, On the Cutting Edge, an archive interview with star Yukari Oshima, Alternate English opening and closing credits and Trailer gallery A second Limited Edition Disc offers HD presentations of the English Export Cut and the all new 'Hybrid' Cut (combining footage from the Theatrical and Extended Cuts for the longest possible version) Now if only Eureka had given this same Super treatment to Eastern Condors instead of relegating it to amongst a three movie boxset largely devoid of extras. Hopefully in time we'll see this remedied as rumours suggest The Criterion Collection have plans to add it to their lineup sometime in 2023. Here's hoping that we can see a truly great special edition of Eastern Condors coming along to sit alongside this epic edition of Millionaires Express.

WINNER - DRAW - They're 100% Identical apart from the Cover Art, Booklet and Menu Screen

Hon Mentions

I'm pretty sure we'll see UK or US releases of The Peacock King and the Saga of The Pheonix coming at some stage, two more Yuen Biao fantasy action films worthy of a mention and for now there are solid HK Blurays of both available from your HK movie store of choice (I recommend DDDhouse) or direct from Panorama HK

I opted not to include the glorious Criterion boxset of Once Upon A Time in China as whilst Yuen Biao is certainly present in the first movie, those films are really more the Jet Li show, so that set is best saved for a Jet Li Special issue someday..

For loads more movie reviews, upcoming Blu-ray release information , unboxing videos and to also be able to chat with other Kung Fu and Martial Arts Blu-ray collectors,
take a minute to jump on over and find me on Youtube, where I post regular updates and new videos every few days.

Written by Johnny 'The Fanatical Dragon' Burnett

www.youtube.com/thefanaticaldragon

THE ART OF DUBBING

BY PAUL DRE

Mark Rolston

Dubbing.... love it 'or' loathe it, it's importance to it's adoring fans in the world of international cinema can never be underestimated.

It's fairly safe to edge a bet that if you to have been a Jackie Chan fan, dating back to the golden VHS era and beyond than

you're no doubt well in tuned with those original export English language dubs that circulated the Western regions and further a field.

Most will have firm favourites that have subsequently become in bedded in their brains for the remainder of their days. For many of us, these English dubs offer a nostalgia dose in abundance and were the voices that we were most familiar with growing up and to some extent pay a fundamental part of our childhood's and attachments to the main man himself.

Now, we know the voices but do we know the individuals behind the voices, the faces behind the 'Jackie' masks.

Sources seemingly confirm that the very original man responsible for first #1 kick starting Jackie's English language export career was Chris Hilton. Chris secured his first Jackie gig by taking the helm (or rather the mic), for the 1979 Soon Lee film company's 'Master with Crack Fingers', in which Jackie's character is called Ah Lung. Not to be confused with the later dub for Dick Randall's 'Master with Cracked Fingers' which was dubbed into english by Larry Dolgin.

Voice actor Matthew Oram entered the stage for a momentary attempt (yes, that's right, just like George Lazenby) in the Golden Harvest export English dub for 'Hand of Death' (1975).

Matthew Oram and his wife were fairly well established regulars in the dubbing circuit of Hong Kong cinema during the 70's and early 1980's.

Chris Hilton soon returned as the original Jackie (yes, that's right, just ike Sean

Connery - you know where this is going!) for the Lo Wei vehicle 'New Fist of Fury'.

Don't panic, Roger Moore soon arrived in the shape of Warren Rooke. Between Chris and Warren, the pair delivered the Jackie voice as we know it for an English speaking market, through the majority of Chan's inventory of 1970's kung fu beat em ups.

Chris Hilton alongside the aforementioned titles went on to voice Jackie in the first export dubs for 'To Kill with intrigue', 'Magnificent Bodygaurds', 'Half a loaf of kung fu', 'Dragon Fist' and 'Snake in the eagles shadow'.

Page 30

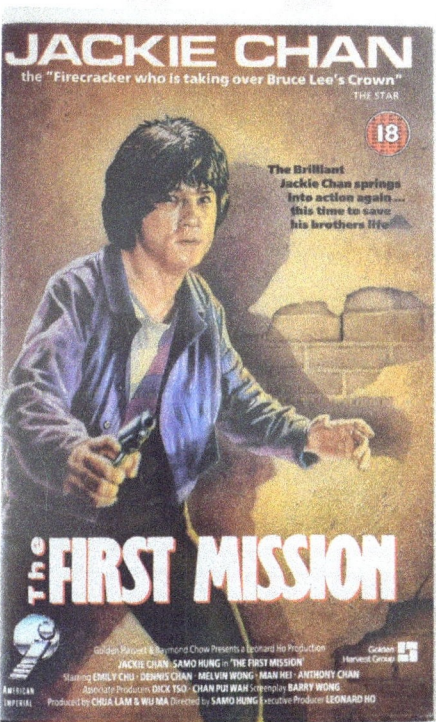

Warren Rooke competed for air time by providing Chan duties on 'Shaolin Wooden Men' (considering Jackie played a mute for the majority of the movie, Warren had ample time to adjust to his new responsibilities), followed by, 'Snake and Crane arts of shaolin', Spiritual Kung Fu and 'Drunken Master' first dub.

Like all good ventures the dubbing duo ventures came to an end as we entered a new decade and Jackie's English was replaced for an 80's audience.

Barry 'Bruce Lee' Haigh stepped behind Jackie's lopping hair for the voice actor responsible for the first english export dubs for both 'Young Master' and 'Dragon Lord'.

The baton was to be firmly passed to two men, who would take on the mantle for 1980's, as previously performed so well by Chris Hilton and Warren Rooke. One of those men happened to be voice actor John Culkin. To Jackie fan's, Culkin will be best known for providing the auditable tones of the original 'Kevin Chan' from the first export dub of Police Story.

John Culkin also dubbed Jackie in the first english export dubs for 'Fantasy mission force', 'Fearless Hyena 2', 'Twinkle Twinkle Lucky Stars', 'First mission' aka 'Heart of the Dragon' and 'Armour of God'.

The second man, unlike all of the above, had a string to his bow like no other. Many

will know his voice recording works, although it is possible few have noted his later connection to Jackie Chan, this man is akin to the Easter egg of Jackie Chan dubbers, lurking in physical presence within Jackie's arsenal of movies.

This man was responsible for serving up the original export english dubs for 'Project A', 'Project A Part 2', 'Wheels on Meals', 'My Lucky Stars', 'Police Story 2', 'Dragons Forever', 'Miracles', 'Armour of God 2 Operation Condor' and 'Police Story 3

Supercop'.
The mystery man returned in the 00's to provide a second redub for 'Drunken Master', replacing Warren Rookes voice.

The face behind the Jackie mask is none other than Mark Rolston. Mark had become the english voice of Jackie behind the scenes for many years, that it was rather surreal to discover him, alongside Jackie Chan in a blockbuster movie.

The movie being 'Rush Hour' in which

Mark plays agent Warren Russ. This marks the first time one Jackie's voice actors was to appear opposite from him in a movie. Mark during an interview made reference to a conversation he had with Jackie on the set of Rush Hour , where he disclosed that he was one of his main english dubbers for his export releases in which a shocked Chan reportedly looked at him in utter disbelief whilst saying "you? No way!".

Mark Rolston although largely unknown to the masses as a regular 80s and 90s era

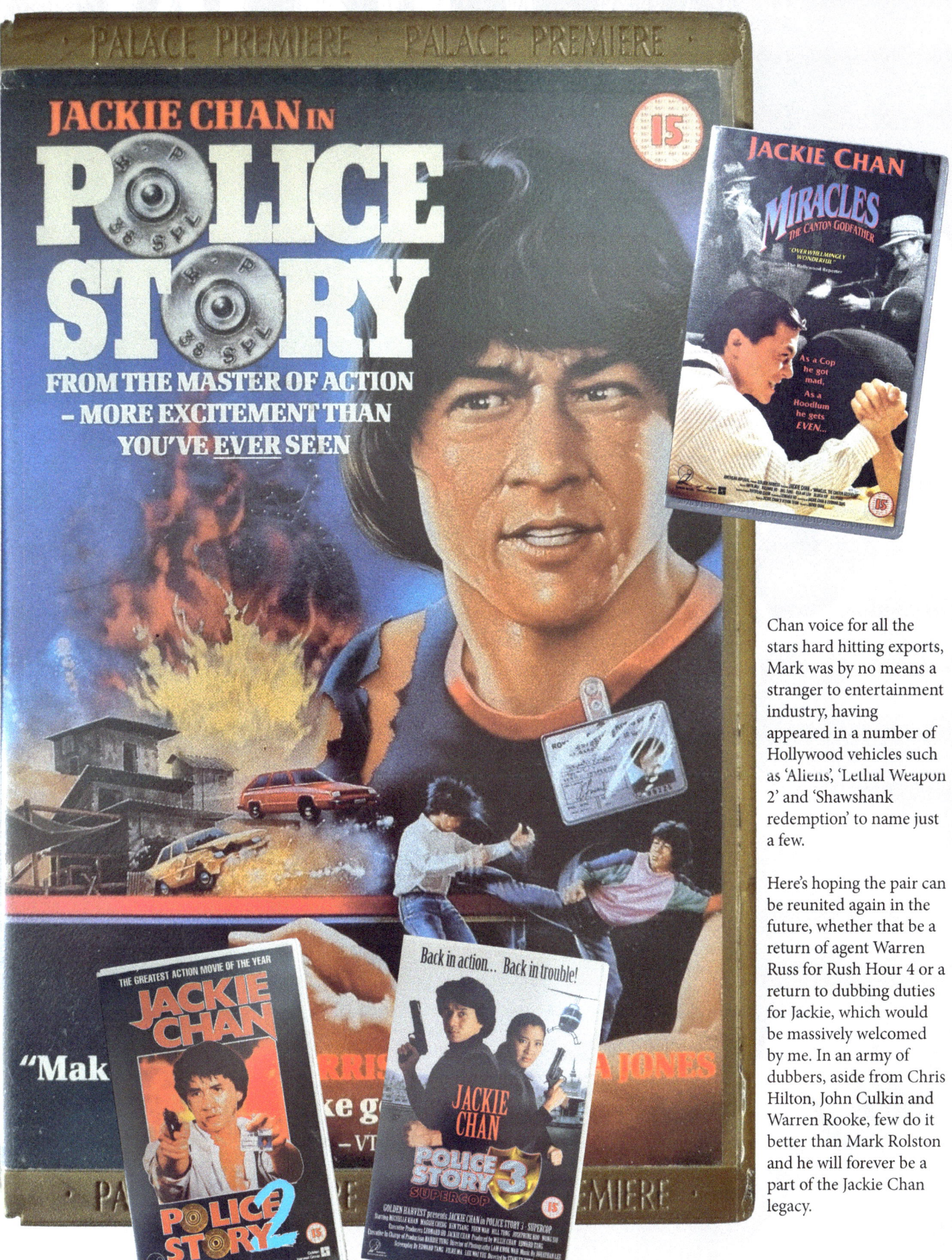

Chan voice for all the stars hard hitting exports, Mark was by no means a stranger to entertainment industry, having appeared in a number of Hollywood vehicles such as 'Aliens', 'Lethal Weapon 2' and 'Shawshank redemption' to name just a few.

Here's hoping the pair can be reunited again in the future, whether that be a return of agent Warren Russ for Rush Hour 4 or a return to dubbing duties for Jackie, which would be massively welcomed by me. In an army of dubbers, aside from Chris Hilton, John Culkin and Warren Rooke, few do it better than Mark Rolston and he will forever be a part of the Jackie Chan legacy.

Jackie Chan
The Lost American Inteviews

By Darren Wheeling

For decades, Jackie Chan collectors and completists all over the world would dutifully record and share his televised interviews, music videos, documentaries, commercials, and other one-off TV appearances via VHS tapes and later DVD-Rs. Most of these TV appearances were never repeated so if you missed it, you missed it.

Finally in 2005, Youtube came along and offered an easier way for fans to share and view these previously rare video clips.

But one historic television appearance, which is believed to be Jackie's first ever televised interview in the United States, has remained stubbornly illusive. The fact that most Americans neither owned a Video Cassette Recorder at the time (nor even knew who Jackie Chan was) resulted in this footage becoming very rare and something of a Holy Grail among collectors.

On July 4, 1979, singer, actress and popular television personality Dinah Shore brought her daily TV program, Dinah!, to Hong Kong to spotlight interesting aspects of life and culture. While there, she visited the newly-built street set of *THE YOUNG MASTER* and interviewed both Raymond Chow and Jackie Chan during the making of his landmark first film for Golden Harvest. The completed program was broadcast once, on US screens to an unsuspecting audience on November 2, 1979. What follows is a transcription of this "lost" interview.

She begins by speaking with Raymond Chow, sitting in director's chairs in the street set of *THE YOUNG MASTER*.

Dinah: This is probably the way a Chinese village looked at the turn of the century. It was all built as a movie set for Golden Harvest studios by the man who discovered the phenomenal and legendary Bruce Lee – Mr. Raymond Chow. Tell me, may I call you Raymond?

Raymond: Oh yes, please.

Dinah: How did you discover Bruce Lee?

Raymond: Well I first saw him in an interview on television in Hong Kong. He did some fantastic things like kicking a piece of board and breaking it in half by dangling it on a string. Not holding it against anything else. So it was really a fantastic feat.

Then by the time I tried to track him down he already returned to the United States.

Dinah: Now, he was born in the United States wasn't he?

Raymond: Yes. He was born in San Francisco, but he was brought back to Hong Kong when he was three months old. And then he spent most of his time in Hong Kong for his primary education.

Dinah: There was a fierceness about him that came through the screen. I saw several of his movies. How many movies did he make for you?

Raymond: Well, he made four and a half.

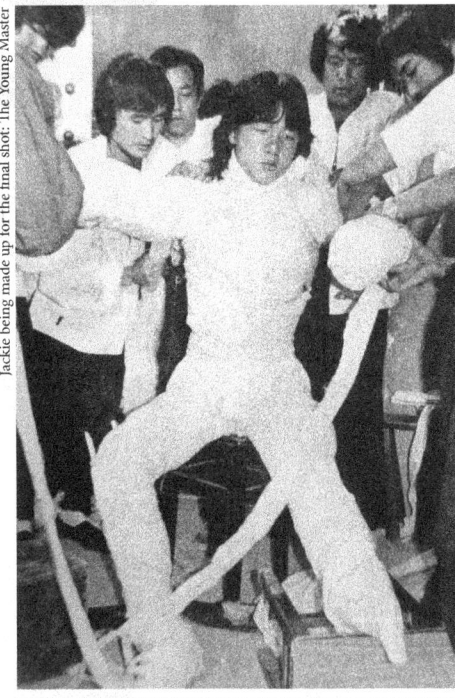
Jackie being made up for the final shot: The Young Master

Yuen Biao & Jackie suffer in the summer heat

Jackie thanks Jimmy Wang Yu for help breaking his contract with Lo Wei

We finally managed to finish the last one, uh, several years after his tragic death.

Dinah: Yes, untimely.

Raymond: It was really a big loss to the whole world. Especially for the movie industry.

Dinah: I had the privilege of seeing two or three of the movies you made with Bruce Lee. But for those people who have not seen them in our audience, we have a little scene from one of his early films. Can you explain this particular scene?

Raymond: Oh yes. This one is from his second film called *FISTS OF FURY*. (sic) In the film that we are going to see, he's trying to break through to a Japanese karate school to find the bad guy. Of course in going through the school, he has to demolish, I don't know how many karate fighters. Let's count them.

Dinah: [Laughs] Bruce Lee.

[Clip from *FIST OF FURY* plays, followed by applause from off-camera audience.]

Dinah: (He) demolished the world. One thing about Bruce Lee. You never say die.

Raymond: Right.

Dinah: You never know when he was licked. What are the differences between movies you make for pure Asian consumption and for the United States' market.

Raymond: For the United States market you really have to spend a lot of time and effort and money to make it bigger than life. As we are going to film a picture called *HIGH ROAD TO CHINA* which is a big, big thing about a girl trying to fly from London to China in eighteen days in 1920. So that is a picture with a large scope.

And *SHIPKILLER 2* is bigger than life too because it's about an ultra huge oil tanker – the biggest in the world, running down a yacht and killing the wife of a doctor. And the doctor seeks revenge.

Dinah: So that sort of handles *STAR WARS* and *GALACTICA* and all of the enormous productions that we're shipping out to the world which are so popular. *SUPERMAN*,

Fred Weintraub, Raymond Chow & Jackie Chan

Jackie, Robert Clouse & Kristine DeBell

that sort of thing.

Raymond: Oh yes. It's very popular in our part of the world.

Dinah: We have a gentleman here that is your latest discovery, making quite a name for himself in Asia.

Raymond: Yes! We have… Jackie Chan.

Dinah: Jackie Chan.

[Applause as Jackie enters and sits down in the empty chair next to Raymond, shaking hands with Dinah]

Dinah: Jackie, you speak English?

Jackie: Sorry, not much.

Dinah: Not too much. So we will have Mr. Chow translate for us. Because whatever you speak is more than I speak of Chinese. Did you know Bruce Lee?

Jackie: Of course.

Dinah: Your personality is quite different from Bruce Lee's. Wouldn't you say Raymond?

Raymond: Yes I think completely different. Jackie usually plays very nice, good natured guy, who doesn't know kung fu in the beginning, like a country bumpkin. Then gets bullied around. In the course of the movie he learns everything and ends up the winner.

Dinah: I have two very good, athletic friends that I've brought with me from the United States who are quite adept at their particular sports. Brilliant athletes both of them. And I thought perhaps if you could choreograph a little kung fu fight for Harvey Korman (American actor and comedian) and for Don Meredith (ex-American football player). It would mean a great deal to our audience to see this sort of expertise.
Would you mind?

Jackie: Of course.

[Jackie gets up and starts "fighting" Meredith and Korman in the middle of the street set, kicking much faster than they can react.]

Jackie & Kristine DeBell

Jackie waiting for his cue

Jackie studies English with his instructor

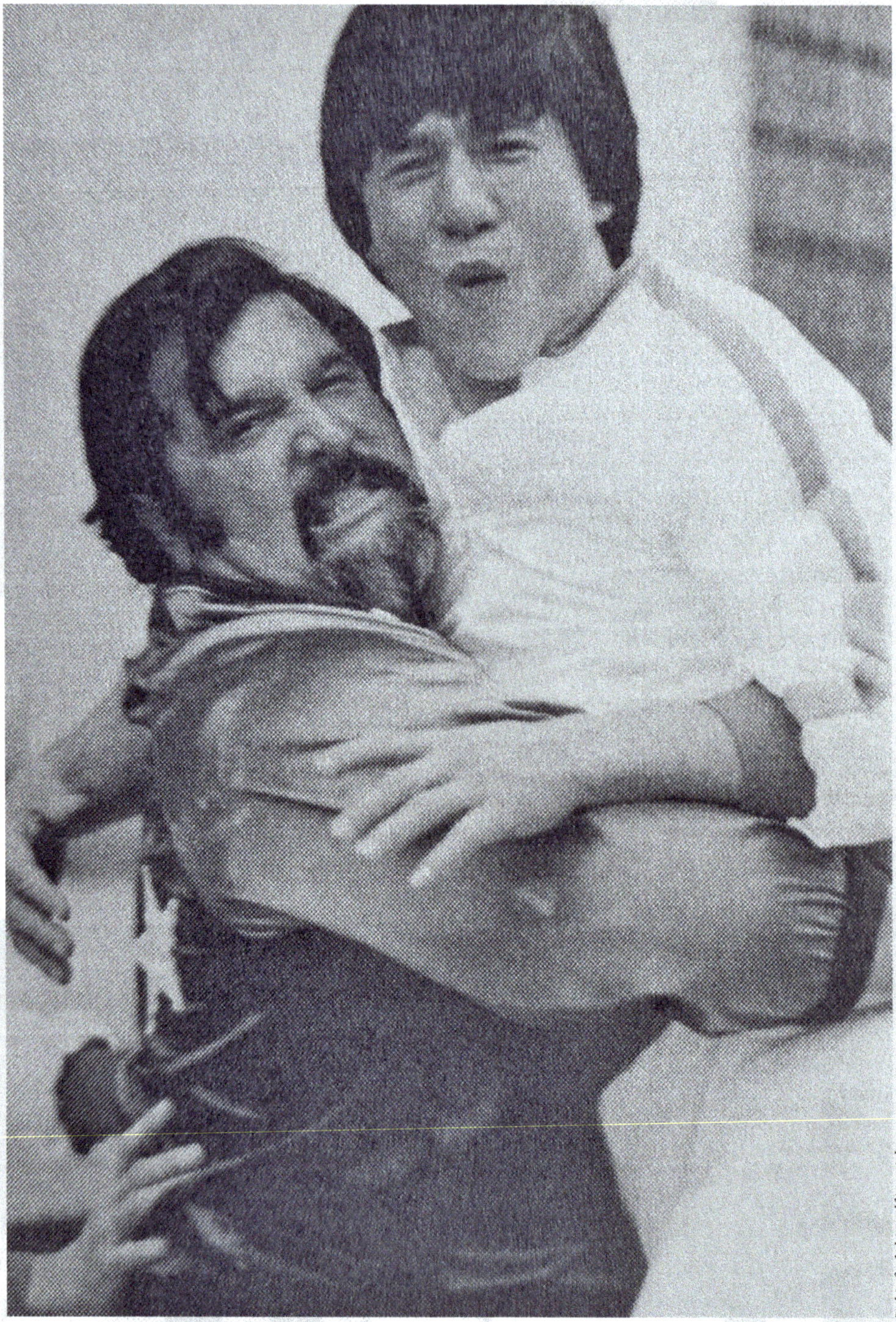

Dinah: Now let's see the other stuntmen do it.

[Jackie and his stunt team run through a group fight in slow motion. He barehandedly fends off five guys with swords and sticks in typical Chan fashion.]

Dinah: Thank you! What a treat. That was really great. We have a clip from Jackie's new movie THE YOUNG MASTERS (sic). We'll see that now.

[Several clips are shown including some footage of a fight with Yuen Biao that was not in the final film. Some of the sound design is different and there is no music.]

Dinah: [Applause] Thank you. I really enjoyed that. [Turning toward Harvey Korman] You were just going to say something?

Harvey Korman: I was just going to say that was great. [Then he sneakily pretends to elbow Jackie in his chest. The audience laughs. Then he says to Jackie, "Try me". Then Chan playfully punches him back in the stomach as he collapses in pretend agony. Jackie catches him as he falls and everyone laughs.] You're gonna see so much Chinese food from a week. [Insinuating he will throw up from the punch.]

Dinah: Thank you gentlemen and most of all thank you Raymond, very, very much.

Jackie finds himself in a tight squeeze

[Everyone shakes hands. Then they replay Jackie's jumping split kick to Meredith and Korman in slow motion.]

In June of 1980 Jackie had completed filming on THE BIG BRAWL (know as BATTLECREEK BRAWL outside the US) and again appeared on Dinah Shore's TV interview program (now retitled Dinah!& Friends) to promote his first American production. This time Jackie visited her Los Angeles studio for the appearance. What follows is a transcript of that equally rare interview.

Dinah: [Turning to Don Meredith who, again, joins her show.] I'm gonna introduce someone we met already in Hong Kong.

Don: Good.

Dinah: You already hit him.

Don: I hit him bad, boy. I wiped him out. Straightened him out.

Dinah: Not quite. I don't know how he's gonna feel when he sees you again. He's the number one box office draw in all of Asia. And I think when the American audiences…

Frank Gifford (ex-American football player): They have more folks than we have.

Don Meredith: They go to picture shows a lot more than we do too.

Dinah: They sure do. But when Americans get a crack at seeing him in a film called BATTLE CREEK BRAWL I think they're gonna fall in love with him too. He's charming. He's open. He, if possible, puts humor and art into the art of kung fu. Please welcome Jackie Chan.

[Applause. Music plays as Jackie enters, everyone stands and shakes his hand before sitting back down.]

Dinah: How's your English?

Jackie: Hmmm, all right. (smiles)

Dinah: Ya know, when we were in Hong Kong, I think Jackie could say "hello" and "goodbye" and that was about it. Not even "nice to meet you." But you're doing much better now they tell me.

Jackie: Uh, after Hong Kong I studied my English seven hours a day.

Dinah: Seven hours a day?

Jackie: Yeah.

Dinah: Lemme tell you something. You can speak English a lot better than we can speak Chinese.

Don: I think you speak English better than I speak English. (Audience laughs)

Dinah: May I, can we, ask you some questions?

Jackie: Yes. Of course.
Dinah: Slowly.

Jackie: Okay.

Dinah: Okay. Your American film is going to be BATTLE CREEK BRAWL. Are you excited about that?

Jackie: (scratches his neck as if confused).

Don: Happy about it.

Dinah: Happy.

Don: Like it

Jackie Oh yes! Very much.

Dinah: See I knew you could act as a translator. (pointing to Don Meredith)

Frank: I'm seeing a first here. Don interpreting. (Audience laughs.) This is a first.

Don: It's what I do every Monday. I interpret. (Referring to his work as a television commentator for Monday night American football games.) What do you think I do? When Howard (Cosell) says something I tell them what he said. (Audience applause)

Dinah: (Turning to Jackie) Let me, I'll explain to you. They are talking about Monday Night Football. Which is not kung fu. Not soccer. It's not rugby. It's not even show busi- I don't know what it is. But it's wonderful. Everybody in America knows about it.

Jackie: Yeah, I like it too. The football like this. (mimics tucking football under arm and running, and blocking with his elbow)

Dinah: You have been labeled as the world's greatest kung fu artist. And Bruce Lee was

your idol before that. Explain kung fu to us will you?

Jackie: Uh, kung fu is a lot of different. Karate, martial arts, (smiles as he struggles for words)

Don: Tai Chi.

Jackie: Yes.

Frank: I covered this on the Wide World of Sports one time.
Dan: Frank can help us.

Frank: And there are all different sort of variations of the martial arts. And kung fu, just to say it, doesn't cover them all. It's almost a spiritual thing. It really is. Almost a religious thing. And the really good people, and I know Jackie is, they are really something, they are almost a notch above everyone in their own society. It's a very spiritual thing.

Dinah: A lot of it is mind over the body.

Jackie: Yes. Martial arts means quick. You learn everything. Like ,uh... When I was young I had martial arts school ten years. Then I don't know, everything. The every day the teacher say "punch". Then I punch like this. Just punch. Then I get more bigger, bigger, Then I know when the punch is turn. Not like this (Jackie illustrates punching straight from his side, then repeating but this time twisting his arm as he extends the punch) When you're bigger, bigger, then you know more, more. When I'm old. Fifty. I still want to learn. Not done. Never.

Dinah: Never really learn all there is. (soft music plays) We'll be right back. That music means...
Jackie: Good! (grabs his chest and slumps back in nervous exhaustion at speaking English live on TV. Everyone laughs and the cast pats him on shoulder telling him he's doing good.)
[Commercial break. Then the program returns.]

Dinah: I'm here with Frank Gifford and Cindy Garvey and big Don Meredith, and we have been joined by Jackie Chan who is learning to speak English for his debut picture, BATTLE CREEK BRAWL. The number one draw in all of Asia.

And we were just talking with Cindy who is a physical arts major. She does all kinds of exercise. Whenever she comes on the show she has to exercise for us. And we were talking during the commercial about the difference between kung fu, which is fast, and tai chi. Would you show a couple

Kristine DeBell, Jackie & Willie Chan

of kung fu moves to Cindy? And show the difference with Tai Chi, a little.

Jackie: Yeah. I first talk first. Tai Chi, everybody think it's slow. So when I was young I don't like to learn because you must learn about ten years, slow. Then study quick, quick, quick. Very difficult. If fifteen years the old men, in Hong Kong a lot of old men you can't touch him. It's fast. Like a ball. When you learn the Tai Chi. Put the ball here. Like this.
[Jackie stands up and pretends he's hugging a ball, rolling it around against his chest.] Then I started to learn quick first. But still slow.

[Jackie moves away from the other guests to give himself some room to showcase some martial art moves.]

Like this. You can see just...

[Chan illustrates some slow arm movements]
No power.

Cindy: But in within two minutes you will be perspiring.

Jackie: Yeah.

Dinah: Jackie, why is it so difficult? Show, what muscles are you using?

Jackie: No muscle. Just relax.

Don: A lot of hot lights. (Audience laughter)

Jackie: Then like this. Like this.

[More slow motion punching. Don stands up as if to challenge Jackie. Then Jackie switches into very fast movements and punches. Don quickly sits back down. And the audience laughs.]

Cindy: Now what is that?

Jackie: That is quick. You just, one...

[Jackie goes thru each movement one at a time. Then strings them together into a blur of arms.]

Jackie: This means. Here. Grab. Here. Then punch.

Cindy: Have you ever hit anyone with your martial arts? With your kung fu?

Jackie: Uh, (smiles innocently) Yeah.

[Everyone laughs and applauds.]

Dinah: Before you sit down can you do a

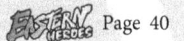 Page 40

JACKIE CHAN IN THE BIG BRAWL

A Martial Arts fight to the finish. Filmed in America by the producers of 'Enter the Dragon'

kata? A kota? In kung fu? A little kung fu. To show the difference. Somebody said kata was…

Jackie: Kata?

[Jackie doesn't understand her request]

Jackie: Cartoon? Kung fu a little different. Some like a tiger. So you should take your time. Some people say what's this? [Performs tiger style arm shapes] No good. You should take your time. About twenty years. But I still don't want to learn. Because you should put your finger like this. [Jams his fingers repeatedly into the floor.] It hurt. [Audience laughs.] Then I don't want to learn. I just want to learn some of this. [Does basic punching arm movements.]

Dinah: Do the kung fu.

Jackie: Kung fu a lot of… tiger. Tiger is. [Does full tiger style pose] Like this. [Fast kicks]

Cindy: Pretty.

Jackie: You should practice every day, like this. You try it. [Chan motions to Don Meredith]

Frank: Now wait a minute. Your body isn't ready for this, Don.
[Don stands up and they both fully extend their arms straight forward and open and close their fists quickly, repeatedly.]

Jackie: Quick.

Don: As quick as I can go man. Those other moves remind me of the east Texas jitterbug.

[Laughter]

Don: He did this to me. Ya know, when we were in Hong Kong, we went out to do that. I almost passed out just from the heat. Remember when we came over to do this. And everybody was jumping on you and you were doing all this sort of stuff.

Dinah: With the knee and the leg. We have a scene from BATTLE CREEK BRAWL. Maybe that shows what we are talking about. Come here. [Dinah motions for Chan to sit back in his chair next to her.] We'll look at your movie.
Don: We'll see a scene for BATTLE CREEK BRAWL. That's up in Michigan.

Dinah: We'll see what happens to you.

[The "Jerry, you must not fight" alley fight scene plays, but with no soundtrack music. Then it cuts back to the studio and the audience applauds. Jackie looks a little embarrassed but smiling. Dinah and her cast rave about the scene amongst themselves as the theme music rises and the show fades to commercial. END.]

COLLECTING JACKIE CHAN JAPANESE MOVIE PAMPHLETS

BY MICHAEL NESBITT

There are many different kinds of promo movie memorabilia that people can collect from all around the world. While most of these collectables follow the same kind of format, they have all become highly collectible. One of the rarer pieces of promo material released for movies was the movie pamphlet, which was also known as a souvenir program or movie brochure. This was a booklet, which was normally A4 in size, full colour, had information about the movie, its cast, and was packed with numerous photographs.

It's interesting to state that the movie brochure first started appearing as far back as 1916, however, with the outbreak of World War II, fewer pamphlets were being produced, due to the short supply of paper. And by the end of World War II, most countries stopped releasing them and concentrated on pressbooks, posters, lobby cards, and other pieces of promotional material to help promote the movie. It was only Japan that carried on the tradition of the movie brochure, and still produces them to this day.

During the past fifty years, there have been many Japanese movie pamphlets released relating to martial arts movies, all of these have become highly collectible, but, the most collectible are the ones relating to Jackie Chan and his movies. What follows is a comprehensible list of all the Japanese movie brochures released for Jackie Chan movies, all of are highly sort out by collectors and are becoming more rare with each passing year.

1976 - Shaolin Wooden Men

1977 - To Kill with Intrigue

1978 - Dragon Fist

1978 - Drunken Master aka Drunk Monkey

1978 - Half a Loaf of Kung Fu

1978 - Snake and Crane Arts of Shaolin

1978 - Snake in the Eagles Shadow aka Snake Monkey   1978 - Spiritiual Kung Fu

1979 - The Fearless Hyena aka Crazy Monkey   1980 - Battle Creek Brawl

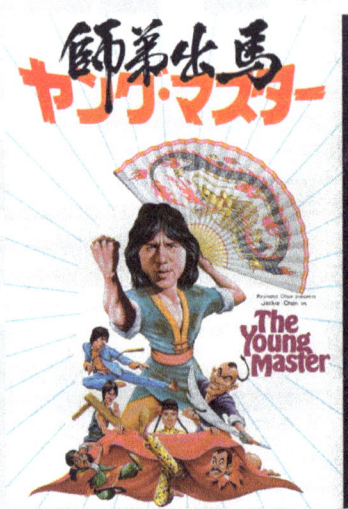  

1980 - The Young Master   1981 - The Cannon Ball Run

1982 - Dragon Lord

1983 - Fantasy Mission Force

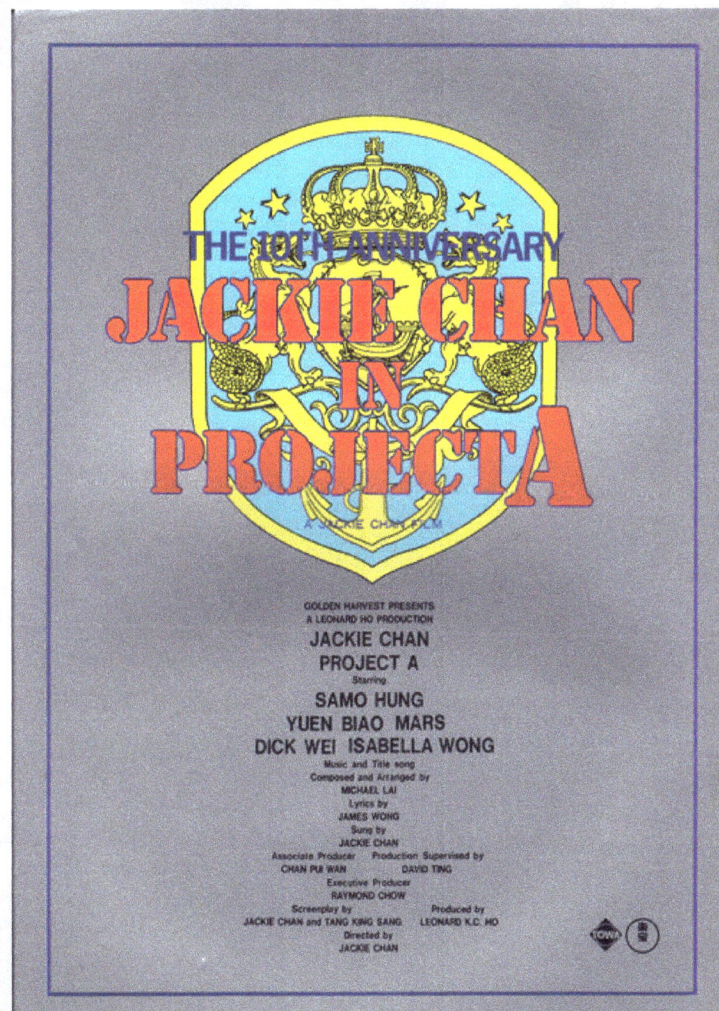

1983 - Project A

1983 - The Fearless Hyena Pt 2 aka Crazy Monkey Pt 2

1983 - Winners & Sinners aka 5 Lucky Stars

1984 - The Cannon Ball Run 2

1984 - Wheels on Meals aka Spartan X

1985 - First Mission aka Heart of the Dragon

1985 - My Lucky Stars

1985 - The Police Story

1985 - The Protector

1985 - Twinkle Twinkle Lucky Stars aka 7 Lucky Stars

 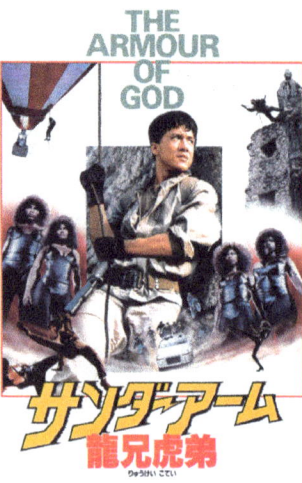

1986 - Armour of God

1987 - Project A Pt 2

1988 - Dragons Forever aka Cyclone Z

1988 - The Police Story Pt 2

1989 - Miracle aka Mr Canton and Lady Rose

1990 - Armour of God 2 - Operation Condor

1991 - Island of Fire

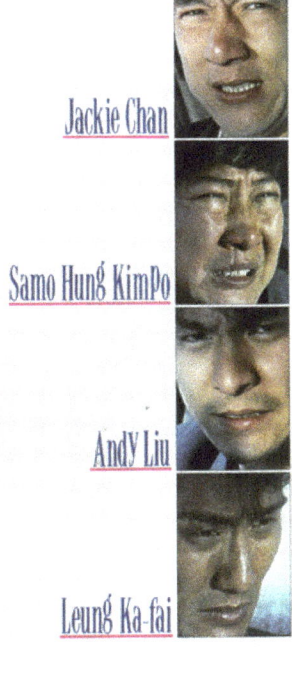

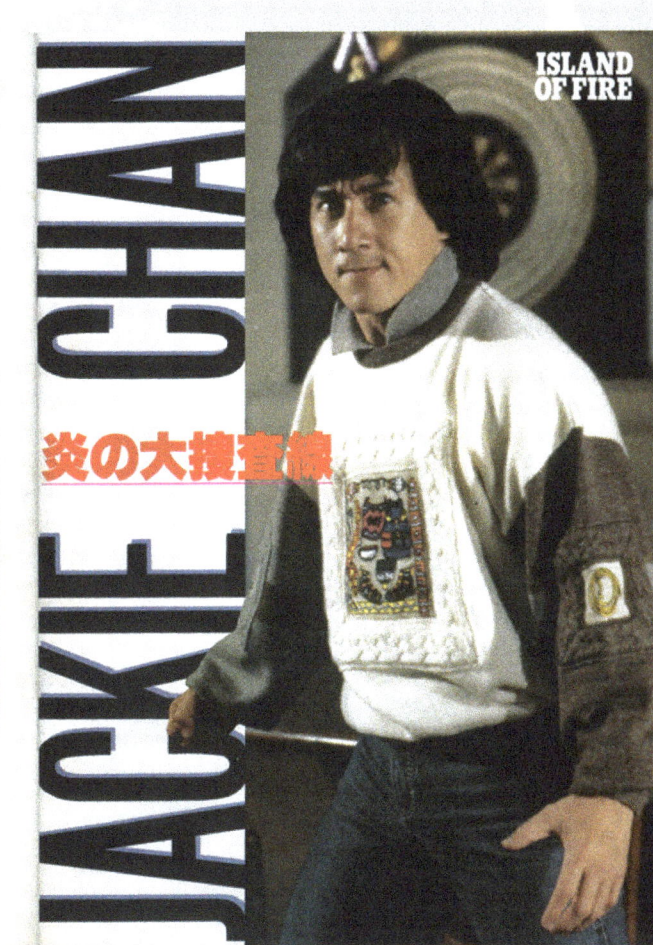

1992 - Police Story 3 - Super Cop

1992 - Twin Dragons

1993 - City Hunter

1994 - Crime Story

1994 - The Drunken Master 2

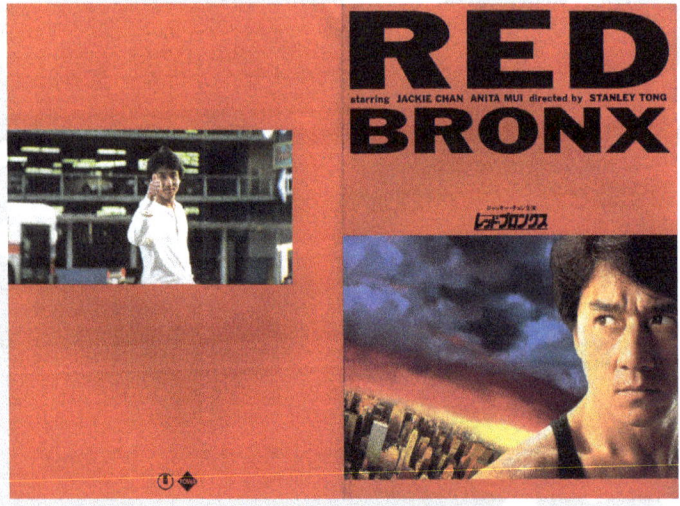
1995 - Rumble in the Bronx aka Red Bronx

1995 - Thunderbolt aka Dead Heat

1996 - Police Story 4 - First Strike

1997 - Mr Nice Guy

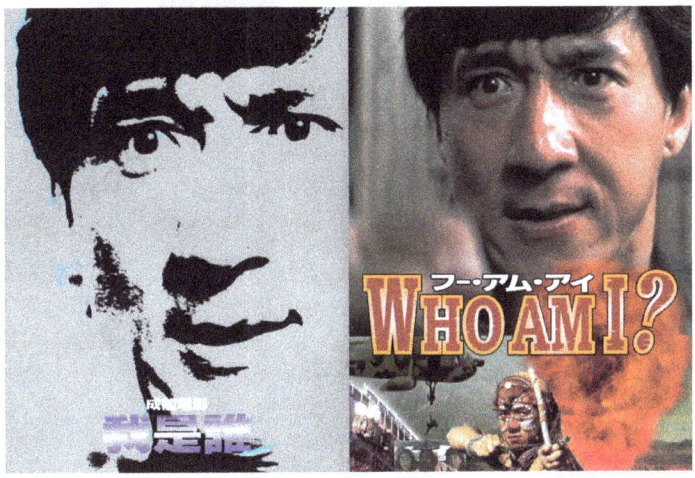
1998 - Who Am I

1998 - Rush Hour

1999 - Gorgeous

2000 - Shanghai Noon

2001 - Rush Hour 2

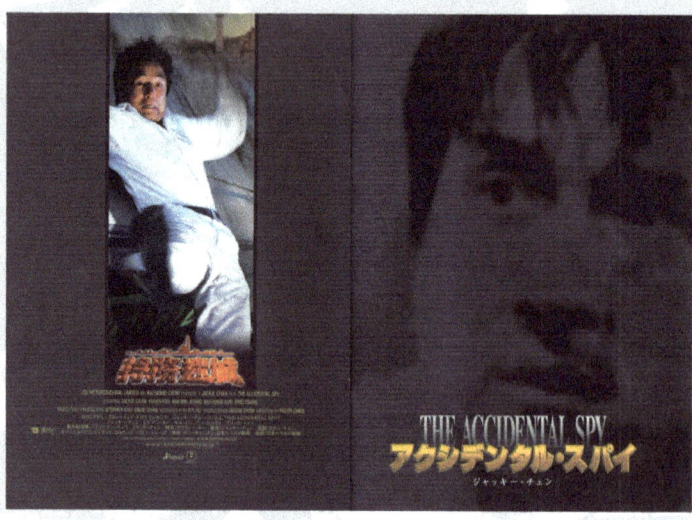
2001 - The Accidental Spy

2002 - The Tuxedo

2003 - Shanghai Knights

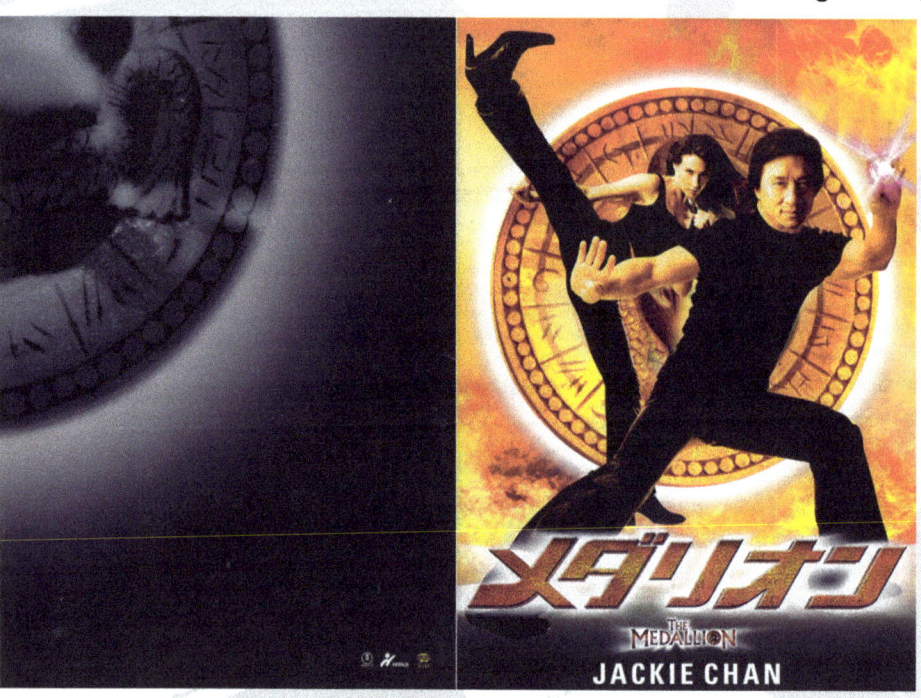
2003 - The Medallion

2003 - Traces of a Dragon - Jackie Chan and his Lost Family - Documentary

2007 - Rush Hour 3

2008 - Kung Fu Panda

2008 - The Forbidden Kingdom
aka The Dragon Kingdom

2009 - Shinjuku Incident

2010 - The Karate Kid

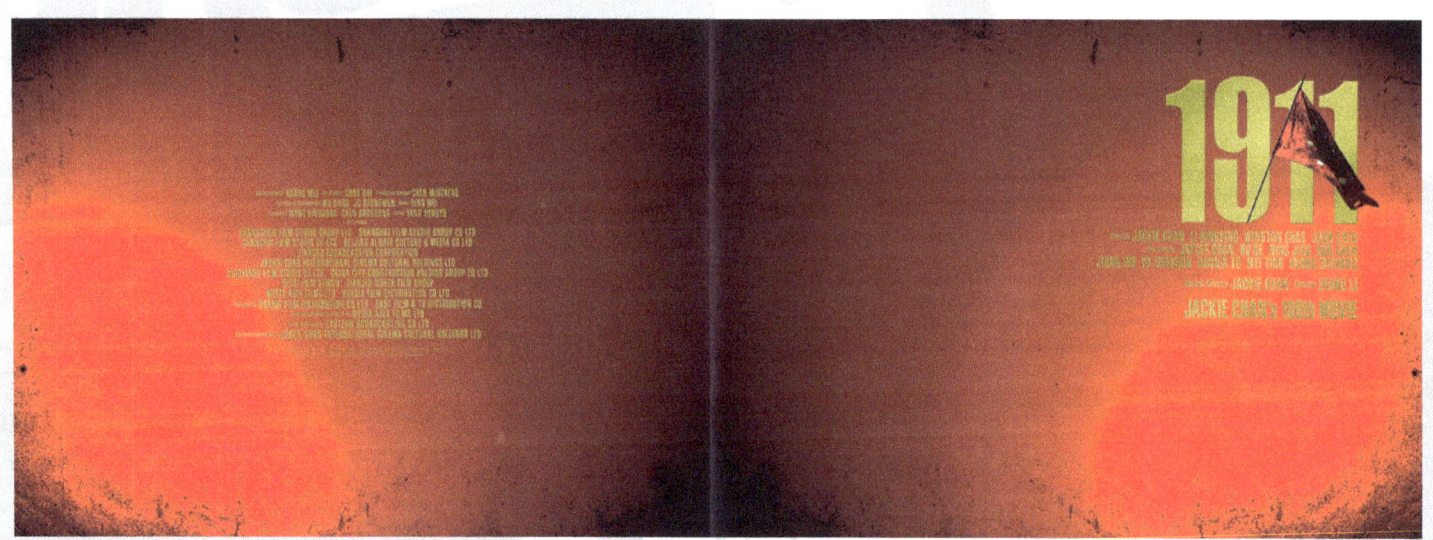
2011 - 1911

2011 - Kung Fu Panda 2

2012 - Chinese Zodiac

2017 - Kung Fu Yoga

2017 - Police Story Reborn - Bleeding Steel

FANS OF THE 36 CHAMBER
INTERVIEW WITH PAUL BRAMHALL
BY ALAN DONKIN

Jed Maxwell: "…It's fans like us that make you what you are."
Alan Partridge: "I don't actually agree with that. I know some people do, but I don't."
I'm Alan Partridge, S1 E5

Sorry, Alan, but your namesake here is one of those fans. It's an old cliché that you're nothing without your fans, but there's truth in it. No matter how talented you are, the fans are the catalyst and fuel that tap into your fledgling efforts and support you thereafter. The same applies to any hobby or interest you'd care to name.

Like any film sub-genre, kung fu cinema enjoys a passionate and dedicated following amongst a relatively small group of hardcore fans. The readers of this very magazine are the people who keep a singular and exciting period of filmmaking alive. As the glory days of peak 'Old School' gradually retreat in the rear-view mirror, we are left with the memories and experiences of those who experienced it comtemporaneously, and those who enjoyed the first wave of home releases and rentals through the development of VHS and other media. Their recollections, efforts and wisdom are invaluable. Like any fandom, however, the torch needs to be kept alive by new fans, including those who didn't experience the initial wave at all. We are all of the same tribe, keeping the scene going through our shared love and enthusiasm.

In an occasional series, I'll be asking kung fu cinema fans about their love for the genre, showcasing (I hope) a wide variety of experiences and thoughts, and painting a portrait of our fandom.

The first person to feature is Paul Bramhall, whose work you may be familiar with. I first encountered Paul's work many years ago, when I realised that some of the random, low budget features I was watching had been reviewed by him. Not just brief, one paragraph summaries, either, but full, detailed, insightful reviews. When I thought about putting together this feature, his was a name that leapt into my head, because you have to be a very dedicated fan to put the effort into writing reviews for films from decades ago that not many people have heard of! There's certainly no 'fame' to be enjoyed from such an endeavour, so I was interested in hearing his story.

AD: Hi Paul. Thanks for agreeing to do this. I've watched kung fu films for years. Maybe about 15-20. But I still feel that I've barely a scratched the surface of seeing what's on offer. How did you get into the genre?

PB: Firstly, the feeling's mutual! I think one of the best things about being a fan of kung-fu cinema is that it's impossible to watch everything the genre has to offer within one lifetime. If you enjoy kung-fu movies, you live with the joyous knowledge that you'll never run out of them to watch. As for myself, I'll soon be able to say I've been watching them for 25 years, and that's partly because I can pinpoint the start of my journey to a specific year.

It was really a case of the planets aligning through a number of factors coming together at the same time, but if I could highlight one event that topped all the others, it would be going to the Odeon cinema in my hometown of Liverpool as a fresh out-of-college, impressionable 18-year-old to watch The Matrix with my mate in 1999. As a first taste of Yuen Woo Ping-choreographed action, our jaws were left on the floor, and we left the cinema in agreement that we needed to see more kung-fu.

Whether or not it was a coincidence I'm not sure, but around that same time a documentary was shown late night on Channel 4 about the Shaolin Temple in China. I distinctly remember a part of the documentary that talked about a movie which was filmed there in 1982, appropriately called The Shaolin Temple. The narrator calmly explained how the movie became famous for kickstarting a wave of wushu mania in the mainland. But, more than anything that was being said, the things that remained lodged in my brain were the clips that played over it from the movie itself.

Bodies flew through the air at each other from opposite directions, clashing against the backdrop of the sky; monks spun themselves up from horizontal positions to land on their feet; and a mass battle played out onscreen, with everyone armed with every weapon imaginable. Despite not having any of the special effects or budget of The Matrix, I found myself sat there feeling the same sense of amazement that I had in the cinema, and knew it was a movie that I needed to track down. As it happened, the expectation that it would be hard to track down what must surely be an obscure title turned out to be a completely unfounded one.

Shortly afterwards, a couple of friends and I found ourselves in the local Blockbuster Video - a store we'd haunt at least once a week. The three of us all loved movies, but you could say we loved them in very different ways, so settling on a title to rent for the night sometimes took longer than the actual movies themselves. I don't remember what we ended up renting that particular time, but what I do remember was that on a small selection of shelves dedicated to VHS tapes you could actually buy, was not only The Shaolin Temple, but also The Shaolin Temple 2, and a third one! I bought them all the following day. The composition of the VHS cover remains with me even now – the image of a monk poised on one foot set against a red backdrop, with the title splashed in large yellow lettering, and the bold declaration written across the top: "Jet Li – Hong Kong's Hottest Action Export". I guessed that's who the monk must be.

It was a bombastic name, and admittedly the only Jet I'd known until that point was the one I'd had a huge crush on from the UK version of Gladiators. Rated 18, there in the corner was the logo of the distributor – Eastern Heroes. Over the coming weeks, my friend and I would watch the complete trilogy, but it was the original one that left the lasting impact. The sequence where Li goes through the seasons performing wushu routines, the scenes of the monks practising on the lawn, and of course, Li in drag. I was hooked, and now, close to 25 years later, I still am.

A lot happened in the 6 months that followed. The year 2000 introduced itself with none of the chaos many expected. I purchased the latest piece of technology called a DVD player, and in February I picked up the debut release of a new DVD label called Hong Kong Legends, which went by the name of Snake in the Eagle's Shadow. Ironically, I didn't buy it because of Jackie Chan, but rather because the back of the DVD case espoused that it was choreographed by "Yuen Woo Ping, who recently shot to fame as the architect of the mind-blowing high-impact fight sequences in Warner smash-hit The Matrix" That guy! Naturally I was sold, and it became the first DVD in a collection which I'd now be fearful to count. The rest as they say, is history!

AD: I love the specific nature of that doorway into the scene. Latching onto a choreographer must be far less common than hunting the filmography of a star! Were you ever tempted to turn your hand to martial arts yourself?
PB: Honestly, no.
Well, let me rephrase. Tempted? Yes – but not to a point where it ever became something I seriously considered. The closest I ever got to actually learning

martial arts myself was during a trip to Hong Kong in 2006. I recall that the now defunct site kungfucinema had posted an interview with Mark Houghton during that same year, and a lot of it was focused on how he was now running a Hung Gar school in the New Territories, and his lineage to Lau Kar-Leung. If it was just a couple of years earlier it wouldn't have meant much, but I'd become aware of Houghton through the Hong Kong Legends DVD releases of Outlaw Brothers and Skinny Tiger and Fatty Dragon, and similarly had become familiar with Kar-Leung thanks to the IVL DVD releases of Shaw Brothers movies. So, it wasn't so much about taking up kung fu, as it was thinking what a cool opportunity it would be to train with a legitimate gweilo bad guy from the movies.

The piece on kungfucinema actually had the school's number, which I called once I was in Hong Kong, and it was Houghton who picked up! Long story short, I spent a day at his school learning the basics of Hung Gar, and being on the receiving end of his formidable kung fu. I will say it gave me a much greater appreciation for the martial arts, obviously Hung Gar specifically. I remember watching Fist of the White Lotus, and there was a move in which Lo Lieh's Pai Mei shrugs off Gordon Liu with a kind of flick of the shoulder, sending him flying. I'd always assumed it was exaggerated for the screen, but part of the alleged basics saw Houghton demonstrate the same move on me, and I distinctly remember being airborne before landing in a crumpled heap. Of course I attempted to shrug it off, while at the same time thinking that this must be why people take kung-fu classes in 1 or 2 hour increments, as opposed to going at it for a whole day.

The ordeal/awesome experience did wrap with him breaking out these massive glass

jars of homemade herbal medicine that I was able to submerge my entire arms into, which definitely helped to ease the pain of punching wooden dummies all day, although they didn't do much for my aching posterior. In any case, that's the closest I've got to learning a martial art. As much as I love watching the action onscreen, that's always where I've been happy for it to stay.

AD: I think you've got to have a certain drive and mindset for anything that requires an intense level of skill and dedication. I tried learning the guitar once, but abandoned it when I realised that actual effort was required. With martial arts, you have the added complication of getting your arse handed to you every other day. I'm too much of a wimp to take that. I'm mightily impressed that you spent the day with Mark Houghton, though, even if you ended up getting brayed. Has your film reviewing led into any other memorable scenarios with people from the industry?

PB: A couple of instances immediately spring to mind.
The first one is actually thanks to Eastern Heroes! Way back in 2014, Ricky Baker had recently resurrected the EH brand, and what better way to come back with a bang than by bringing Hwang Jang Lee over to the U.K. for a talk and seminar!? As someone who was still in school during the Eastern Heroes peak of the 1990s, when he'd brought stars like Jet Li and Chow Yun Fat to British shores, I recall feeling distinctly envious that such an event was happening again, but since I was now living in Sydney, it'd be impossible to attend. Through a series of serendipitous events, I ended up being in Denmark on a business trip the week before, so decided to extend by a couple of days, and booked a flight to London from Copenhagen leaving first thing Saturday morning.

At that time I'd only been writing for City on Fire for 6 months, so I somewhat over-seriously (I blame it on my excitement level) reached out to Jeff and asked him if he'd mind if I attend in the capacity of representing the site, and if he'd be ok with me using it as leverage to try and secure an interview. Of course, he was cool with it. I mean, what Asian cinema site is going to say no to the chance of securing an interview with one of the greatest boot masters to grace the screen, but for some reason I felt like I should ask. I contacted Ricky directly, and he very kindly organized a 30-minute slot (which ended up becoming 1 hour) for me to sit down with the Silver Fox one-on-one. It was a surreal experience, and despite the ridiculously early flight and coming directly from the airport, I'll always consider that interview as one of my first 'scoops', one which to this day I still can't quite believe. I got to sit down with the villain from that very first HKL DVD I picked up 14 years earlier.

The second situation took place the following year. When Hong Kong Legends released The Scorpion King (or *Operation Scorpio* as it's known in the U.S.) on DVD in 2002, like most people, I was mesmerised by the performance of another Korean boot master, this time in the form of Won Jin. The rules of gravity really didn't seem to apply to this guy! Researching about him back then, there was all kinds of rumours – from having one of his legs amputated, to such extremes as he'd died! Skip forward to 2015, and I'd noticed he was featuring in a new movie in his native Korea called Kwon Bob: Chinatown. Being a frequent visitor to Korea (thanks to my better half being Korean), and still riding the high from the Hwang Jang Lee interview, I decided to try my luck and see if I could get a Won Jin interview the next time I was there.

After connecting with him on Facebook of all platforms, he said he'd be happy to meet, so it came to pass in September 2015 that I found myself sat in a quite café in a Gangnam backstreet with Sunny the Scorpion himself sat opposite me! Again, it was another surreal experience, and he hadn't lost a touch in being able to bust out the moves, even throwing out the classic

A STING IN ITS TALE...

A CITY ON FIRE INTERVIEW WITH WON JIN "THE SCORPION KING"
BY PAUL BRAMHALL

scorpion pose amidst sips of coffee (the café was really quiet!). The funny thing was that we ended up talking about how myself and my then fiancé would be returning to Korea the following year to get married, and he said it'd be an honour if we'd invite him to our wedding. I recall sitting there thinking to myself, here's Won Jin, the guy who I've watched onscreen countless times, saying it'd be an honour if we'd invite him to our wedding, when I'm pretty sure the honour would be ours if he'd say yes to it!

Sure enough, the following year I can say that Won Jin was one of the guests at our wedding. Whenever I look at the photo album of the day, of course first I look at my wife, and then second, even if it's just in my head, I'm thinking "there's Won Jin just casually mingling at our wedding!" Since then, whenever we come to Korea, my wife and I always catch up with him over a coffee somewhere in Seoul. Unsurprisingly, I can also say that every time we do, I think to myself that if someone had told the 21-year-old me when I bought The Scorpion King DVD in the local HMV that, 20 years later, I'd regularly catch up with the guy on the cover over coffee in Seoul, I'd probably have thought that they had a few screws loose. Having said that, that someone may have had an even tougher time convincing my 21-year-old self that I'd one day be married, so I guess everything is possible.

AD: That's an incredible story, Paul. You hear about some stars doing things like that (I'm sure Keanu Reeves has turned up at someone's wedding that he met in a hotel bar), but rarely encounter it in real life. Now I can enjoy that experience vicariously through you! Returning to your entry into the world of kung fu cinema, was there any star that you had a particular love for at the start of your journey?

PB: It wasn't so much a specific star, as a specific label. The combination of getting into kung-fu cinema at the dawn of the DVD era, and also living in the U.K., pretty much saw me picking up every Hong Kong Legends title as they were released. I think the benefit for someone like myself who got into the genre during those years, is that the special features the DVDs came with allowed a relative newcomer to become quite knowledgeable in a ridiculously condensed period of time. Thanks to the Bey Logan audio commentaries that usually accompanied each title, and the interviews with many of the cast and crew that were similarly included, each release became as much about receiving an education on kung-fu cinema as it did about watching the actual movie! Even today, with labels like 88 Films and Eureka! cranking out awesome Blu-rays of many of the same titles, I've never been able to bring myself to part with my HKL DVDs.

As a result, you could say I organically developed a love for Jackie Chan through being exposed to his best work from two decades over just a couple of years, but when it comes to someone whom I proactively looked to watch the filmography of, then the first would be the Shaw Brothers director Chang Cheh. I'd first read about him after picking up the book Mondo Macabro by Pete Tombs in the early 2000s, but at the time it was almost impossible to access the Shaw Brothers library. I was intrigued by the way he was described as the 'Godfather of Kung Fu Cinema', and the description of his movie Crippled Avengers sounded completely out there and like nothing I'd ever seen before. Ironically, when IVL started releasing the Shaw Brothers catalogue in 2003, one of the first titles I picked up was Heroes Two, purely based on thinking that the cover looked cool, and not actually realising that I'd unintentionally chosen my first Chang Cheh movie.

After that I picked up close to every Chang Cheh title (a few slipped through the cracks) that hit the shelves over the next five years, and never failed to be entertained by his filmography. Well, with the exception of Magnificent Wanderers. That was awful. There was something about the unashamed machismo of his productions that made them seem like they took place in another world from the (mostly) 80s and 90s Golden Harvest titles that I'd been accustomed to until that point, and I knew I needed more! More is definitely what I got, and I'm embarrassed to say I still have DVDs from that era which haven't made it out of the factory seal.

AD: Snap! I've still got a couple of dozen during my initial three-year splurge that haven't escaped the confines of their shrink-wrap straitjacket. The thrill of collecting in that early period is one that was both intoxicatingly intense and infuriatingly difficult to recapture. Some days I was having deliveries of five DVDs; other times it was a drip, drip, drip of daily deliveries.

Over the years I've tried to catch up on the ones I bought but didn't watch. After each viewing, I tend to google the film to survey the thoughts of others. I've lost count of the number of times that the first

meaningful, in-depth review I've clicked on has been one of yours on City on Fire. How, and why, did you start to enter the world of reviewing obscure, low budget epics produced 50 years ago?

PB: Appreciate you reading them! For me, I've always enjoyed writing, so this story probably makes sense to start back when I first got into kung fu cinema, and I stumbled across the now defunct (and appropriately titled) kungfucinema website. By the time it was the early 2000s, and sites like hkflix and cdwow suddenly opened up a whole new world of being able to import DVDs not only from the States, but from Hong Kong itself, it was Mark Pollard's insightful reviews on kungfucinema which informed a lot of my purchases. Looking back now, I'm surprised I wasn't bankrupt by 2005. During those formative years I never thought to try my hand at reviewing myself, since I was still very much learning about the genre, but after spending 3 years in Australia I returned to the UK in 2007, and felt confident enough to e-mail Mark to see if he'd be open to having me onboard as a guest reviewer.

I submitted a review for Mercenaries from Hong Kong as a sample of my writing, so was over the moon when he got back to me and said he enjoyed my review, and would be happy to have it on the site. You could say that was the original kickstarter that gave me the motivation to continue. Unfortunately, Mark stepped away from the site not long after, and in the hands of the new owner the focus turned away from old school kung fu flicks, and became predominantly about 80s and 90s American DTV action movies, which I wasn't really into. In the end, my reviews for Mercenaries from Hong Kong and Long Road to Gallantry made it onto the site. However, looking back now, I'm kind of glad they're no longer available. I recall my writing style back then was very plot heavy, as in I'd spend 4 to 5 paragraphs just detailing the story, when really all a review needs is the synopsis like you'd get on the back of a Blu-ray case.

After that, you could say I got out of the reviewing game almost as quickly as I got into it, instead choosing to post my musings on the Kung Fu Fandom forum, which back then was a part of the kungfucinema site. It was in March 2014, when the hype was building up to the release of The Raid 2, that a Sydney-based forum member made a post, saying they had a couple of tickets to an advance press screening which had been forfeited by colleagues who couldn't attend, so they were being offered up first come, first serve. It was literally screening just a few hours later, but having relocated back to Sydney a couple of years prior, I immediately cancelled the plans that I had and said I'd be happy to take them off his hands. Thankfully I got in before anyone else (a benefit of many forum members being U.S. or U.K. based), and after roping in a mate to come along with me, that evening we got to be some of the first to check out the sequel.

It was an awesome screening, with everyone left in awe of what they'd just witnessed, and despite finishing the night off with a few beers, once I got home I went onto the forum and excitedly typed out a few giddy paragraphs sharing my thoughts. I woke up the next day to a message from Jeffrey Bona, the gentleman who runs the City on Fire website, asking if I'd be open to having my comments from the forum used as a review for The Raid 2 on COF, since it'd be considered a kind of scoop to have an early review for such a highly-anticipated movie. I said I was cool with it, and probably the reason why I'm still writing for COF close to 10 years on is due to his response back – he replied obviously saying thank you, but then asked me if I'd mind "tidying it up to make it sound a little less fanboyish"!

While I'm sure some people could have been offended by the request, for me it was a sign that said: here's a guy who

wants quality writing for the site he runs, and not just any old crap (like a bunch of excitable paragraphs written while semi-intoxicated). I duly obliged, and later we got into a conversation where I mentioned I'd be up for providing more reviews if he'd be up for posting them, and that's how my relationship with COF started. Especially now, there's not too many sites left providing purely written content for, as you refer to them, "obscure, low budget epics produced 50 years ago", and while I don't purely review kung fu movies, part of what I love about writing for COF is that there's no restrictions on what gets reviewed. It can be the latest Chinese blockbuster, or some Taiwanese kung fu movie shot in a forest in 1970. Everything's game, and that's what keeps it enjoyable for me.

AD: That's a fascinating journey, and we owe Jeffrey Bona a debt of gratitude for his 'open door' policy to films that no-one else gives houseroom to. I think I speak for all old school fans when I say that I'm glad that you had the opportunity to bounce back from the 'false dawn' you endured earlier in your career. The Raid 2 is a fantastic film, and I can see why you went all 'giddy fanboy' on it.

I found that when I went through my kung fu cinema journey, I had an early love for shapes films. From there, I branched out to wuxia swordplay's (mostly from Taiwan). Eventually, I began to appreciate what were known as 'bashers'.

Did you embark on any particular journey, beyond the films you've mentioned already? I remember that, for years, I refused to watch bashers, because I considered them to lack finesse. I didn't want to watch anything that had a modern setting, because martial arts should possess a more mystical element, more suited to long grey hair, robes and jade jewellery. I'd rather watch a schlocky cut and paste than a new wave classic. I didn't watch many 'big' films, because I figured that they'd be there forever, and I'd rather experience the thrill of finding a little-known gem. It's been a long path of discovery, with my ignorance being shamed regularly!

PB: I guess my journey was kind of the opposite of yours, in that I started with a 4th generation VHS copy of a movie like The Dragon Lives Again on a Video Asia Bruceploitation 4 pack.

There was no quality control, and I think I became a bit of a snob towards certain subgenres, which was compounded by the fact that so many of the available titles were presented in such shoddy quality. People may have their complaints against the Hong Kong Legends and IVL Shaw Brothers releases of the era, but comparative to the average release from Ground Zero or Hollywood Video (remember them?), it was like watching a movie which had been made yesterday. So I'd say I didn't particularly prioritise any specific type of genre, but definitely

Chiba, and that The Streetfighter trilogy was going to be receiving a DVD release, I was all over it. Upon watching them, my mind simply couldn't adjust to the karate-style action aesthetic, and I found them to be epic disappointments. These days I can appreciate Takuma Tsurugi for the unapologetic bad ass that he is, but back then, I was left bewildered as to why anyone would recommend The Streetfighter movies.

I definitely understand the thrill of uncovering a hidden gem though, with some of my favourite kung fu movies being ones which I hunted down based purely on seeing a brief clip in a fight compilation, or mentioned in a throwaway line in a

what's considered to be the cream of the crop - so the 'big' films that you're probably referring to - but the downside of such an approach is that early on it led to me watching a lot of movies that I wrote off as rubbish, only to re-evaluate many years later. Like I mentioned before, with the number of titles that became accessible through sites like hkflix, I soon found myself following the They Live mantra of "consume" on a constant mission to fulfil my kung fu itch. The result, though, sometimes meant that I'd watch a digitally remastered (this was long before 2K and 4K scans!) version of a movie like Dragons Forever thanks to Hong Kong Legends, then follow it up with a blurry, ripped from

looking back, on reflection many of my opinions were informed on making unfair comparisons to what was available at the time.

For the longest time I refused to watch any Bruceploitation movies (blame that Video Asia 4 pack). However, now I have an appreciation of the genre, from Dragon Lee's wild yelps, to going so far as to say that some entries are genuinely solid kung-fu flicks like The Gold Connection and Bruce and the Iron Finger. Similarly for many Japanese movies, my initial viewing habits had led me to unconsciously expect every Asian action movie to be like a Jackie Chan flick, so when I heard the hype around Sonny

discussion. I still recall seeing a clip from the Taiwanese movie 21 Red List on a YouTube fight scene compilation, and after much research I uncovered that the only place it'd received a DVD release was in Taiwan, which sent me on a frenzied hunt! I eventually tracked it down, and the thrill of watching the movie for the first time is one I wish I could rediscover all of these years later!

AD: It seems like we have taken very different paths in that regard! I developed a love for the trashier films from the off, thanks to catching them on various satellite channels. The person who collected Hollywood East? That was me. I didn't

They're premium products, but packed with neat extras and features.
As you know, I collect various king fu cinema-related memorabilia. Other than film releases, have you ventured into other areas of collecting in the genre?

PB: Yeah I've seen your impressive collection of posters and lobby cards, it's quite the treasure trove! As for myself, trust me, if you saw my Blu-ray and DVD collection, you'd understand why the answer is a hard 'no' when it comes to expanding into collecting anything else!

AD: I can sympathise with that! Collections just seem to swell to gargantuan proportions. What would you consider to be your favourite films in the genre?

PB: I was fearing this question would come up because it's so difficult to answer, but since I've asked it to people myself, I'll have a crack at listing 10 of my favourites! My only caveat would be that if you ask me

mind the fuzz, or the pan and scan, or the fact that sometimes one of the 'special features' included on the DVD was 'chapter selection'. I still bought HKL and IVL releases, and could see the difference, but the allure of the obscure was often so great that I have stacks of superior releases unwatched. I didn't even mind DVD-R rips from old 4:3 vhs tapes, where the burnt-in subtitles were chopped at either side. It was all part of the magic. I'd stepped into a different world, and I loved the more difficult to find, grubbier recesses of it.
I can entirely relate to your experience of 21 Red List. For me, it was Sword of Justice. I saw a clip in a trailer for future Rarescope releases on YouTube. Two swordsmen, on a bridge, in the rain, holding umbrellas. It appealed to every sinew of my soul. Imagine my disappointment to find that its planned release had never come to fruition. Then imagine my excitement when I got an email from Jamal in Germany to say that he was organising a fundraiser for its release! I was all over it, and it didn't disappoint in any way whatsoever.
From what you've said, then, I guess that you have a formidable collection of DVDs and Blu-rays?

PB: Ha ha, if you're a kung-fu cinema fan you can only hide from the fuzz, pan and scan, and those deluxe chapter selection special features for so long, before they catch up with you. By the time I'd come to appreciate a guy like Dragon Lee in the 2010s, I found it somewhat ironic that I found myself tracking down budget Hong Kong Connection DVDs on amazon and eBay, that just a few years earlier I could have picked up for £1.99 by strolling down to the local Pound King. But that's life! My physical media buying habits have definitely curtailed over the years, although considering how much I used to buy in those early days, even my curtailed collecting habits may seem incomprehensible to the average Netflix viewer! Thankfully I'd no longer consider parting ways with $100 for an out-of-print DVD (but don't worry, I can say that the time I did it wasn't a Hong Kong Connection release).
But I won't avoid your question any longer. Yes, I have a pretty formidable collection, spread across two countries no less! I think the fact that I got into the genre at the start of the DVD era has meant that the appeal of buying physical media has never really diminished, at least for me, even if the space to store them definitely has. I still enjoy the thrill of a new package arriving in the mail, and while I'd like to follow that up by saying that the thrill continues as I rip off the factory seal, as you already know, that part may not occur until a few years later.

AD: So many companies are pulling out all the stops now, with these luxury Blu-ray releases. I must confess that they've rekindled my interested in physical media.

again in a couple of weeks, the answer may have completely changed! In order of oldest to newest –
The Duel (1971) – While this wasn't the first Iron Triangle movie I saw, it was the first one that I felt had a truly epic scope through its story and characters. The rain-soaked finale and use of Stauss's Sprach Zarathustra are a combination that's likely to be forever etched in my memory!
Knight Errant (1973) – I've always had a soft spot for Jimmy Wang Yu, and this one is my go-to if I need a slice of Jimmy action. Offering up a ferocious face-off

between Wang Yu (with both arms!) and Yasuaki Kurata, and an ending that never ceases to surprise, the result is pure basher excellence.

The Gold Connection (1979) – I love it when directors not normally associated with the kung-fu genre take it on, and this Kuei Chih-Hung slice of Ho Chung-Tao starring grit is the perfect blend of crime thriller meets kung fu flick.

The Loot (1980) – To me this is the ultimate shapes fest. Phillip Ko Fei has never looked so sublime, and it feels like barely a few minutes go by without another awesome display of kung fu goodness breaking out, making it one of my most re-visited 'fu flicks.

Kung Fu Zombie (1980) – Say what you want about the insane undercranking, but I love it, and when it involves a plot that has Billy Chong going up against a blood sucking Kwan Yung-Moon (who isn't averse to kicking people's heads off either), for me you have perfection.

Mirage (1987) – Despite a flimsy plot, this is a movie that contains so many fights and insane stunts that whatever deficiencies there are in the storytelling hardly matter. Also, Yu Rongguang didn't headline nearly enough Hong Kong movies, so when he does, it's a treat.

Swordman 2 (1992) – This was my first real taste of the short-lived new wave wuxia genre that dominated the early 90s, and I was left aghast at the spectacle and complexity of the wirework on display, which made me an immediate fan of the genre.

Drunken Master 2 (1994) – Everyone has that movie that they show to their friends to try to get them into the kung-fu genre, and for me this is the one. Every fight scene is top shelf, and the Jackie Chan vs Ken Lo finale is a pure adrenaline rush.

21 Red List (1994) – A dose of Taiwanese madness where every fight is full of wince-inducing impacts and falls, topped off by having the laws of gravity and physics simply not apply, and why not? The result is one of the most entertainingly high impact fight flicks I've seen.

Wu Xia (2011) – It's perhaps not a surprise that a Peter Chan directed remake of The One Armed Swordsman starring Donnie Yen and Jimmy Wang Yu turned out to be such a cinematic treat, and the fantastic fight scenes in this one are simply the icing on the cake.

AD: There's a nice balance of sub-genres

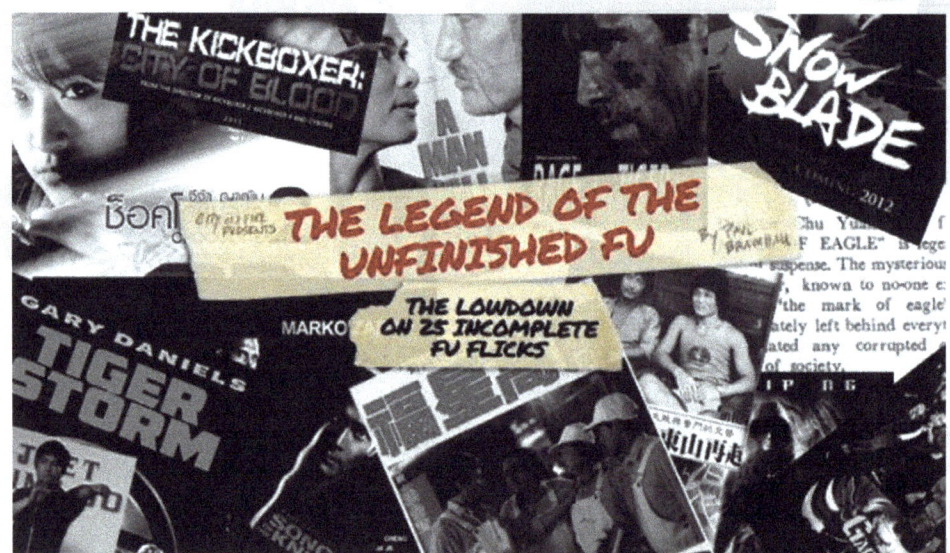

and time periods there. I'm glad you said The Gold Connection. I have to confess that, when I went on a Bruce Li viewing spree a few years ago, I didn't anticipate much. Several of his films were surprisingly good, though, with The Gold Connection being my favourite of the lot. It's so gritty, downbeat and shocking. A genuinely unexpected treat.

On the flipside, are there any films that you've either downright disliked, or felt that their positive reputation was unwarranted?

PB: There aren't too many films which I'd say I plain hate, however the one that will always spring to mind is 1977's Return of Red Tiger. It's actually quite a recent watch as well, the result of the lockdown most of us found ourselves in at some point during 2020, which had driven me to explore some of the darkest recesses in those budget 50 kung-fu movie packs that we're all guilty of owning. I think we all went through moments of delirium during those months, and when I stumbled across a 70s Korean kung-fu flick which had imported Bruce Le as its star, I figured it may have been a hidden gem.

Upon watching Le as a mute beggar who's taken on the characteristics of a traumatised cat, complete with rampant milk guzzling and wild meowing at the sky, I felt genuinely traumatised at the end of it, and to this day it remains the only movie I've given a 0/10 rating to over at City on Fire. I know it's usually Le who catches the most flak out of all the Bruceploitation stars, but I find his latter era stuff like Bruce Strikes Back, Ninja Over the Great Wall, and Black Spot to be solid entertainment,

CITY ON FIRE PRESENTS
Enter The Dragon
The Most Overrated Kung Fu Movie Ever Made?

BY PAUL BRAMHALL

and had always found myself coming to his defence. However, after watching Return of Red Tiger, I know it's only been 3 years, but I just haven't been able to bring myself to champion his corner like I used to since then.

In terms of overrated stuff, if we're talking strictly about movies then, dare I say it, Bruce Lee? I know it's probably partly down to me not being around during the era they were released in, so I realise I won't have an appreciation of just how big of an impact they had at the time, but as movies I just don't find them that entertaining. I think we saw glimpses of what Lee was capable of in the Game of Death footage, which for me showed the most potential of Lee's screen fighting aesthetic, and who knows, if he'd lived, maybe his 'Lo Wei era' would be held in the same regard as Jackie Chan's? As it is though, for someone who's entry point into the world of kung-fu cinema was late 1970s Jackie Chan and Yuen Woo-Ping, while I appreciate Bruce Lee's movies as the landmarks that they are, they're not productions which I ever find myself craving to re-watch.

Can we include a "Paul is exempt from being cancelled" clause at the start of this interview please?

AD: I fear that horse has bolted. The sound of sharpening pitchforks and blazing torches is echoing around fandom…

I do understand where you're coming from. He was one of a small group of stars whose films enjoyed a worldwide reach, opening the floodgates for the genre. I do like his films a lot, but sometimes find myself wondering what classics we've been denied. I understand that Rebellious Reign was written for him? That's an incredible film and one of my favourites, and if it represents the standard of films he could have starred in during the mid-to-late 70s and early 80s, then we've been denied some true classics. I would have loved to have seen him in a shapes film. Or a wuxia. Early 70s films in general I have a healthy respect for, but most of my favourites come from later dates, and it's mostly down to fight choreography preferences.

Of course, none of this will prevent this quote from becoming legion: 'Dare I say it … Bruce Lee is overrated.' Perhaps get a t-shirt made?

Returning to your writing, what is your writing process? I ran a blog for a couple of years ages ago, and mine involved making notes while watching the film. I'd then write up a review, snapping screenshots from the film to illustrate various comments. The upside was that I provided raw, unfiltered opinions. The downside was that I spent far too much time fussing over notes and not enough time immersing myself in the film. If I had the time, I'd have watched the film once, with a beer, then rewatched it with a pen and notepad.

PB: I'll contact Ricky and see if he'd be willing to sell the t-shirts through Eastern Heroes. I'm sure they'd be a popular choice! As for my writing process, it's very similar to yours, but minus the screenshots. I'll use the notes feature on my iPhone to quickly type shorthand observations while watching a movie, usually of stuff that I feel will be important to include in the review, except, of course, if I'm watching it in the cinema. After 10 years of reviewing, I find I can quickly make notes now, while still being able to immerse myself in what's onscreen, even with a beer, so for me it's gotten to a point where there's no longer really a line between watching a movie for enjoyment and watching one for review purposes.

Again, I think that really comes down to the level of freedom I have at City on Fire when it comes to reviewing. I can say in those 10 years that I've never reviewed a movie because I have to. It's always been something I've done willingly. I'm sure for 99.9% of reviewers writing for sites that focus on Asian cinema, there's zero money involved in the endeavour. If you consider an average movie is 90 to 120 minutes long, and for me, at least, the review process takes around 2 hours - that kind of time investment needs to be something you enjoy. So, if that means passing up advance screeners of the latest big budget Mainland war blockbuster, or saying no to the countless offers to interview Mark Dacascos (seriously, I can't bring myself to interview a guy for movies that I've described as the equivalent of a lobotomy), then I feel no sense of loss over it.

At the end of the day, I write because I enjoy it, and the moment I don't enjoy it, I'll stop. If people enjoy reading my opinions then that's great, and I love nothing more than engaging in a conversation as a result of my thoughts, but I never expect anyone to avoid a movie based on my opinion of it. I think most distributors have a similar understanding, as thinking back to the 2014 live action version of Lupin the Third, that was the first screener I ever received. I remember e-mailing Jeff and basically saying I thought it was complete garbage, so asked if I should still write a review or just let it go. He said go for it, and actively encouraged ripping it apart, because in the end there's no such thing as bad publicity. Now I realise it's true - to give a movie coverage and call it rubbish is still better than not giving it any coverage at all, so it's a win-win - I don't compromise my integrity, and the distributors get coverage for their movie.

Of course, if it's a low budget epic from 50 years ago, then such considerations never mattered to begin with, so everything is fair game!

AD: I think it's great to have such a valuable resource on the internet. Are there any reviews you're particularly proud of, or enjoyed writing more than others?

PB: I wouldn't say I'm proud of any reviews. I mean, at the end of the day they're just someone's opinion. The only difference between me and most other people is that I find enjoyment in taking time to put mine into writing. I guess I'm more proud of some of the lengthier features I've written, as they tend to also involve a lot more research, and I enjoy shining a light or putting a new perspective on aspects of the genre which may not have been considered before. The pieces I did around Jackie Chan and Stanley Tong's collaborations, the many action movies that were cranked out by Koreans in America during the 80s and 90s, and Yuen Biao's filmography in the 90s all took a while to complete, and I can say I'm happy with how they turned out.

As for if I enjoyed writing some reviews over others, I tend to enjoy writing all of them, but I confess there's something particularly cathartic about unloading on a movie which I felt was irredeemably bad. Before I started to write reviews, if I watched a particularly awful movie, it'd feel like I'd lost 2 hours of my life, and while it may seem counterintuitive to then spend even longer on the same movie by reviewing it, there's something gratifying about being able to have a rant through the written word. The same is true on the opposite end of the spectrum. The funny thing is, that while I'd never expect anyone to not watch a movie just because I'd given it a bad review, if I watch a really good movie, it's the opposite. My hope is that the

CITY ON FIRE PRESENTS JACKY CHAN "CAMEO STORY"
HIS TOP 10 HONG KONG CINEMA CAMEOS
BY PAUL BRAMHALL

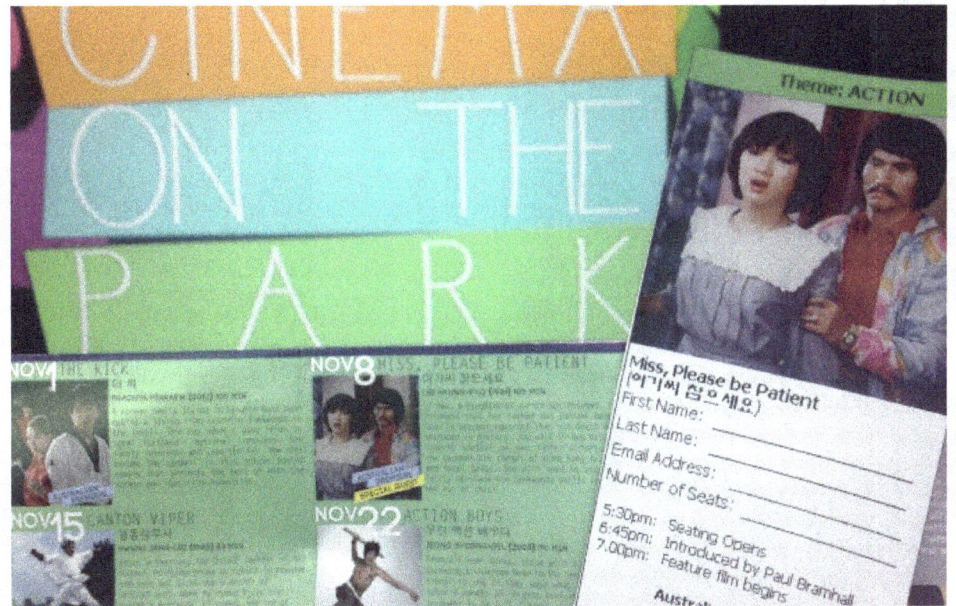

review will turn people onto it who perhaps wouldn't have checked it out otherwise.

AD: I suppose that carries a little extra responsibility with it. I've lost count of the times I've tried to explain to someone why a certain film is worth their time, and failed miserably. Finally, presumably, as a 'newer' fan like myself, then you rue the fact that you missed the glory era of theatrical releases. Yet we are in a period where premium, extra-filled Blu-rays are increasingly frequent. Do you have any ambitions to get involved with these, should the opportunity arise?

PB: Actually, I'm already working with the 88 Films label. I'd originally connected with them in 2020 through a mutual acquaintance, who'd advised that they were looking for support to subtitle some Korean language footage for their release of Spiritual Kung Fu, so you could say that was my first real credited work on one of their titles. It wasn't until this year, though, that things expanded a little, when I started working with them to create content for the booklets they usually include on their special edition releases.
I wrote the booklet notes for their release of God of Gamblers, and I have upcoming features scheduled to be included in their releases of The Untold Story, Twin Dragons, and Battle Creek Brawl, which are all due to hit the shelves at some point in 2023.
It's been a fun journey to push myself out of my comfort zone, and delve deeper into the world of Hong Kong cinema probably more than I've ever done before, so my only hope is that the fans who buy the releases enjoy the booklets that I've written for them.

AD: That's great news. Watching all that dross has certainly paid off!
Thank you so much for being interviewed for this first 'fan feature' article. I hope all of your future endeavours are as successful as your past ones.

Paul's work can be found at *https://cityonfire.com/author/paul-bramhall/*

RIDE ON

BY SIMON PRITCHARD

The synopsis

The Trinity CineAsia UK press release describes Ride On as:
Action legend Jackie Chan (Vanguard, Rush Hour, Police Story) is back in an action-packed and heartwarming tribute to the world of stunts which made him an international superstar.

Luo (Chan) is a washed-up stuntman whose glory days are long behind him. When his trusty stunt horse, Red Hare, becomes the target of debt collectors, the pair fight off the attackers, with their impressive display caught on camera and the video going viral. Meanwhile, Luo works to reconnect with his estranged daughter and her boyfriend, who both take an interest in the legal case against Luo. But when his renewed fame scores him a once-in-a-lifetime opportunity, will he finally put his family first?

Written and directed by rising filmmaker Larry Yang (Mountain Cry) and co-starring Liu Haocun (Cliff Walkers) and Kevin Guo (Adoring), Ride On is a fast, funny and uplifting story of family, with stunning action choreography paying homage to the classics of Jackie Chan.

The premiere

Ride On premiered at the V.U.E. cinema at Leicester Square, London on the 7th of April 2023. The event also fell on Jackie's birthday which made the event extra special. The event opened a couple of hours before the film started; upon entering, we were greeted by the delightful Trinity CineAsia staff. Trinity CineAsia had a massive birthday card that they will present to Jackie. All guests and staff got to sign it. Crazy to think that Jackie himself will be reading

our comments.

We went to the top floor, screen nine, where they had a bar, large promotional posters and a wall of TVs showing the promo material. It was nice to catch up with friends, some from the monthly Eastern Heroes Café, and finally to meet Toby Russell and Mike Fury.

Before the film started we had introductions and stories from Trinity CineAsia. The highlight was a pre-recorded video of Jackie speaking to the London audience. Jackie then repeated the same message in Mandarin. All speech would be in English then in Mandarin, the fluency and ease at which the speakers could switch between languages was phenomenal.

The vibe in the room, the build-up, everyone was excited for this. The premise of the film is simply 'A guy wants to keep his horse and reconcile with his estranged daughter' Whilst this does not sound like the 'usual Jackie Chan' film, it worked phenomenally.

The film seems to be a metaphor for Jackie's life. A reflection on his career and his realisation of the world around him today. Jackie is part of a dying art of stunt performers that goes back to stars such as Buster Keaton and Charlie Chaplin, who did it all for real. With the world around him being overtaken by CGI, health & safety advisers, and new filming methods, his art is becoming redundant.

His love of art and his unwillingness to want to change is shown in his relationship with his horse, Red Hare. The realisation that he is getting old and cannot do stunts forever, mixed with the world around him progressing without him, is representative of his relationship with his daughter, and the struggle between the two.

This film is a roller coaster, with some genuinely funny scenes and poignant moments. "Don't try to push Red Hare through there!!!!" damn. This film will attract mainstream filmgoers to serious Jackie fans. This film is also full of "Easter Eggs", cameos, references to his classic films, and more. The film got a round of applause at the end and people tried to compose themselves before leaving.

I met fellow guest, Wanyin Zheng, who

kindly gave us her perspective on the film.

SP: How is Jackie Chan perceived in China?

WZ: Jackie Chan is perceived as proud of the Chinese. I am not sure about his career. But he is viewed as a pioneer in promoting Chinese action movies, Chinese martial arts, and also Chinese culture to the world at a time when the field was mostly taken up by those who were born and raised in the West. I think most Chinese are proud of having him represent China, or even Asia, on the international stage.

Most of the audiences are moved by his spirit of dedicating himself to producing action movies for many years. Because at present, the Chinese mainland entertainment industry is filled with young actors and actresses who do not have any strengths, passion or experience in acting but still got the chance to lead in TV series or movies, as they have good-looking faces and fans who can ensure nice box office returns.

SP: What were your expectations before the film?

WZ: I did not expect much before the film. I watched one or two of his film(s) when I was in middle school. The martial art he performed is pretty cool as it is usually the highlight that makes people feel thrilled. But I have to say, at least for me, scripts of a large part of action movies follow a very similar logic. It's usually about saving lives, saving the earth, love, hate, reunion and a happy ending. So I did not expect much as I thought that it would be a movie that barely differs from those I've watched before.

SP: What did you think of the film and its highlights?

WZ: I think it is way beyond my expectation as I've cried several times when I was watching. The plots that look back on his career life as a Kung Fu stuntman have really moved me. He has been devoting himself as a stuntman since he entered the field. And the job, I think, is quite unique in the Hong Kong film industry. As a stuntman, he/she needs to consume his/her body and youth to dedicate himself/herself to the art of film. However, they usually don't get fame or money as their shots in the movie usually move fast. Most of the time, people

won't care about who performs this but what they have performed.

Jackie, a very famous actor who is now 69 years old, refuses to use computer-generated shots and insists on performing martial arts by himself. This is not only the spirit of a Kung Fu stuntman, but also the spirit of every man and woman who truly love the things they are doing.

SP: Has this film attracted you to more Jackie Chan films or old-school action films?

WZ: Not really because I am not that into any type of movie. But as I just said, as the movie is far beyond my expectation, it has actually attracted me to Jackie Chan himself, especially his early career experience as a stuntman and how he made his way.

SP: Thank you for speaking with us. Is there anything else you would like to add?

WZ: Fighting Eastern Heroes Magazine!

Ride On is coming soon to Blu-ray, DVD and Digital from Trinity CineAsia.
https://trinitycineasia.com

FILM REVIEWS
by Justyn Hughes

龍拳 (1979)
Dragon Fist
Box Office: HK $1,004,276.2

Dragon Fist was originally made in 1978, but wasn't released until 1979, after Jackie Chan had been loaned out to Seasonal films. At the time Director Lo Wei was having problems with the productions and lack of money, but after the success of Snake In The Eagles Shadow and Drunken Master, he released Dragon Fist to capitalise on Jackie's new found fame.

Jackie Chan plays a more serious role this time round. Playing the character Huo Wan, the movie begins with his master Sam Taai being challenged by rival master Mr Chung (Yen Shi Kwan), after being honoured "Supreme Martial Artist" by local schools. Mr Chung explains he can't be the best, If he hasn't defeated him first. Mr Chung wins the fight, rips down the schools sign and walks away, leaving a beaten and defeated champion to die.

After the passing of the master, Mr Chung is home and finds his wife has killed herself, leaving a note explaining he only killed because she was in love with Sam Taai many years ago. She thinks her death will mean no revenge will be taken further down the line. Huo Wan, takes his masters wife and daughter (Nora Miao) away from the school in search of Mr Chung to take revenge. Arriving by boat, Huo encounters a local gang trying to harass them, this quickly turns sour and Jackie is able to showcase his talents for the first time. Here Jackie is Fast, powerful and too much for his opponents, with great hand to hand combat to defeat them (Nice side angles and long shots).

We are introduced to a third clan "Ngais" who have been having problems with Mr Chung and his students for a long time. After hearing Mr Chung killed Sam Taai and that his student is in town looking for revenge, they see this has an opportunity to try and rough the feathers more and maybe use Huo to their own advantage.

Huo Wan arrives at Mr Chungs school to take revenge, but the meeting is then cancelled for three days leaving Huo confused. After leaving, one of Mr Chungs men (James Tien) followed them home and poisoned the tea, which his maters wife drinks and suddenly falls Ill. Huo quickly learns the identity and challenges him to a fight outside. Once again, great choreography by Jackie, with some nice wide shots so we can see the skill and timing of both him and James Tien. (My personal view of course, but James looked at his best when working with Jackie on screen, also see there fights together in Spiritual Kung Fu).

After three days, they return to speak to Mr Chung, only to find out there can be no fight, due to Mr Chung chopping his leg off after he killed Sam Taai and the death of his own wife. He explains he is full of guilt and this is the only way he can apologise and hopes to move forward from this. Great scene here with both Jackie and Yen showing the audience the emotions felt during the exchange by both men.

Afterwards, Huo takes his masters wife to the doctor, he explains she has an illness he cannot cure quickly and would cost a lot of money. He explains to get paid that kind of money, he would need to work for the Ngai clan. This plays into the clans hands, has now they can use Huo to do there dirty work.

After doing several jobs for them, he quickly realises that what he is doing is wrong and only benefits them. During this time, we have twists and turns with Mr Chungs two best fighters wanting there own fame. They take sides with others also, killing some of Mr Chungs own men to start a bigger feud between each clan. When the clans finally come together at the

end, Huo at first teams up with the Ngai clan, believing his masters wife was taken hostage by Mr Chung, not realising Mr Chung had nothing to do with it, but was his two students and the Ngai clan.

This finale is one of Jackie's best from the 70's, showcasing his many skills from hand to hand combat, kicks, acrobatics, weapons, the lot. The relentless attacks on the whole Ngai clan is reminiscent to something you'd see in a Bruce Lee movie, fast, powerful, bloody and deadly.

This was different for Jackie at the time, mainly using slapstick comedy during his previous films, trying his best working under Lo Wei but failing at the box office. But I'm happy Jackie tried a role like this and feel he could have done more like this during his career. Dragon Fist is one of the better Lo Wei movies, good plot, plenty of fights and a great finale. 88 Films released the Blu Ray a few years back but are expected to re-realise again later this year with improvements to the picture quality. One to grab for sure.

醉拳 (1978)
Drunken Master
Box Office: HK $6,763,793.4

When Drunken Master was released in 1978, Jackie Chan had just exploded on too the big screen with the classic Snake In The Eagles Shadow. Both movies made with Season Films and with Director Yuen Woo Ping at the helm, 1978 was the most vital year in Jackie Chans career. Drunken Master was a big success on its release and widely regarded as a classic in this genre.

Jackie Chan plays the famous Wong Fei Hung, a younger and more mischievous character who likes to cause trouble and chase women. One day on the market stalls, Wong starts to flirt with a young woman and sneakily gets a kiss on the cheek, until the her mum (Linda Lin Ying) appears and teaches Wong a lesson in manners. This is a great scene, Wong telling his friends he can get the girl, only to be dismantled within seconds. Linda Lin gets to showcase her skills, very flexible, performing kicks and the splits with ease.

Wong Fei Hung runs off and then gets into more trouble when he defends a stall holder from being taken advantage off by a local school. This scene really shows Jackie's ability to deliver a perfect blend of action and comedy, a trade mark he held throughout his amazing career.

Unbeknown to Wong, the lady is actually his Aunt and Wong gets a beating by his father for his actions. The following scene is the famous horse stance sequence, with cups of tea placed on his head, arms and legs and cannot drop them. (This was something Jackie would do when he attended peking opera school as a young boy). But Wong still cannot stay out of trouble, trying to get away with free food and alcohol at a local restaurant, then fighting, Wong Kei Ying (his father) decides to send Wong Fei Hung to be punished by Sam Seed, an old drunken beggar.

Wong Finally meets the beggar, and his quickly defeated by him and taken back for the punishment to begin. Wong tries to run away, but doesn't get very far when he runs into Thunder-leg, played by super kicker Hwang Jang Lee. Hwang Jang Lee is always in great form, showcasing his excellent kicking techniques. Thunder-leg defeats

Wong easily and explains that his martial arts is useless and can never defeat him. Wong finally crawls between his legs and his humiliated, forcing Wong to go back to Sam Seed. You can see and feel the pain going through Wongs face and the musical score really brings this scene alive with the audience feeling that pain.

This is when Wong Fei Hung and Sam Seed start to develop a friendship, so Sam Seed takes the training even further and you can understand why is he also has a reputation for crippling his students. What follows is one of the most famous scenes in any Kung Fu movie when Wong Fei Hung is performing up side down sit-ups, transferring water from small cups into big pots, amazing scene. This is what is truly missed from todays Kung Fu movies, fantastic training sequences.

After defeating a gambling cheat in the market place, Wong is send by Sam Seed to fetch some alcohol. Whilst Wong is gone, Sam Seed is attacked at his home by the gambling cheats master, without his alcohol he doesn't have his strength. Wong returns but the alcohol has been switched to water, so Both Sam and Wong Fei Hung escape to fight another day. Sam decides to teach Wong the eight drunken gods, whilst having the Chinese folk song, "Under the General's Orders" playing, something which has been associated with Wong Fei Hung movies for many decades.

Wong Fei Hung heads out to find "King Of Sticks", played by the great Hsu Hsia, who attacked him and his mater at there home. Jackie uses his drunken boxing, a bench, even pushing Hsu face first into dog poo to defeat him. Great scene.

The finale of the movie is a true show stopper, Jackie Chan and Hwang Jang Lee once again face off with Jackie's eight drunken gods vs the undefeated contract killer Thunder-legs. Wong Fei Hung learns his father has a hit out on his life and arrives just in time before thunder-legs kills him. Wong had perfected seven of the drunken gods, but not yet Miss Ho, a drunken woman who flirts her way to victory. This makes for some very funny moments, especially with thunder legs looking on, confused to what is happening.

Jackie Chan really is in fine form here, you can see why after making Drunken Master, he would go on to become one of the greatest of all time. Hwang Jang Lee is superb as always playing the villain of the movie and with Yuen Woo Ping sprinkling his magic, Drunken Master is truly a classic. Jackie would go on to make Drunken Master 2, 16 years later in 1994 and revised the drunken beggar role for himself in the movie The Forbidden Kingdom.

If you haven't seen Drunken Master yet, be sure to grab the Eureka release, which has both Blu Ray and the Dvd in one set.

笑拳怪招 (1979)
The Fearless Hyena
Box Office: HK $5,445,535

After Jackie Chans success with Seasonal Films (Drunken Master and Snake In The Eagles Shadow), it was time for him to direct his first movie, Fearless Hyena. He went back to Lo Wei with more power and confidence than before and was given the reigns to direct and showcase his ability.

The movie begins with the leading villain Jen Tien Hua (Yen Shi Kwan), attacking and and killing members of the Xing Yi School for refusing to join him. He is looking for Ching Pang Fei (James Tien), who is in hiding but trying himself to dismantle Jen Tien Hua and his clan. His grandson Chan (Jackie Chan), exposes a few cheats when betting on the street. The gang don't take lightly to this and attack him, but he quickly defeats them. This is Jackie starting to come alive more with his own style of Kung fu comedy, especially after the success of Drunken Master. Something we didn't see as much during his previous work with Lo Wei.

When Chan goes back to his grandfather, Ching Pang Fei knows he has been fighting and decides to teach Chan how to defend himself, but only to defend himself and not cause trouble. Chan isn't really into learning Kung Fu and would rather goof about and gamble, but gets a job as a coffin maker by the undertaker (Dean Shek). Chan is followed by the men who tried to con him out of money when gambling, they explain there master Tee Cha wants Chan to defend there school from others and will pay a good sum to do so. Tee cha is an unskilled leader and cannot fight off any challenges, so Chan agrees and this is where the movie really starts to pick up the pace.

It isn't long until the first challenge is accepted and Chan gets to showcase his skills using the Bench (something he used later in The Young Master, Drunken Master 2 and more). But Chan has to fight in disguise, so word doesn't get back to his grandfather, but with each fight, he keeps asking for more money has the challenges gets tougher. During one fight, chan's grandfather is watching on, discovers he is in disguise and punishes him for fighting.

Jen Tien Hua and his men are still out looking for Ching Pang Fei, beating people up, even killing them if they don't speak on his whereabouts. He then arrives and speaks to Tee Cha, who quickly tells him the whereabouts of Ching Pang Fei. He arrives at his home and challenges Ching to a duel, killing him in the process. Chan is watching on and tries to help, but is held back by Unicorn (Chen Hui Lou), explaining he would also be killed if he tired to help. Chan is distort by the death of his grandfather and seeks immediate revenge, but unicorn stops him from leaving and decides to teach Chan his Kung fu. (Unicorn being an old friend of his grandfather).

What follows is some excellent training sequences, Chan once again performing the hanging upside down sit-ups like he did in Drunken Master but this time taking it to the next level. We even get to see a chop stick duel between them both, something which was brought back for a scene in Kung Fu Panda.

One day, Chan is sitting with his hands on his head thinking about his grandfather when he see's Jen Tien Hua and his 3 fighters walking by. Chan attacks Jen but is quickly beaten and this shows Chan that he isn't ready yet to take revenge for his grandfathers death. Afterwards, unicorn decides to teach Chan "Emotional Kung Fu", forms that were adapted from the Iron Wire Fist. Happiness, Laughter, Anger, Sorrow and more will be needed to take on such a formidable foe in Jen.

The final 15 minutes of the movie is none stop Kung Fu, with Chan taking on Jens three bodyguards, displaying some unbelievable timing during long, wide shots to

capture every movement. Taking them on not only one by one, but three on one using there weapons against them to kill them off. The finale between Jackie Chan and Yen Shi Kwan will have you reaching for the rewind button. Like many of Jackie's fights, we see his character having to take some gruesome beatings before coming back to save the day. This is something the audience can relate too, someone who maybe isn't the toughest, but the will to win at any costs pushing him on to victory.

Jackie really does showcase some of his best martial arts during these fight scenes, close combat, kicks, weapons, everything. The movie is truly Kung Fu comedy at its best, although not my favourite Jackie Chan Kung fu movie, it certainly delivers with excellent action choreography by Jackie Chan. I really enjoyed seeing James Tien playing on the same side as Jackie this time, instead of fighting each other. James Tien always looked at his best when working with Jackie Chan, he really does get to shine on screen in each of Jackie's movies.

Be sure to grab the UK Blu Ray, looks amazing.

少林木人巷 (1976)
Shaolin Wooden Men
Box Office: HK $476,950.7

Shaolin Wooden Men was the third movie from Jackie Chan in 1976 with Lo Wei. Starring in "New Fist Of Fury" and "The Killer Meteors" previously, Shaolin Wooden Men gave Jackie the chance to showcase his amazing abilities on screen, with great results.

This time Jackie Chan plays "Little Mute", a student of the Shaolin temple. Like his fellow Shaolin brothers, Mute has to injure some gruesome training, like walking with iron shoes whilst carrying buckets of water. Other students like to make fun of him, until one day he meets "Five Plums", a friend of the Shaolin Temple. She gives him advice on concentrating his mind to over come the pain and push forward to become a better person.

But little mute keeps having flash backs to when he was younger, when he witnessed his fathers death by a masked attacker. One day, he meets a drunken monk who leads him to a cave, where inside he meets a prisoner (Chin Kang) chained up. Mute offers the prisoner food, showing kindness, but this is only because he learns the prisoner is actually a deadly Kung fu master and wants to become his student.

Little Mute spends his time going back and forth from the temple to the prisoner for more training. Whilst training, little mute meets Five Plums once again, who explains what he has learnt is for killing, not for self defence and agrees to help him. Little Mute takes all the help he can get, training day and night, dedicating himself to become the best he can be, before taking on the challenge of the Shaolin Wooden Men. We get to see some great training sequences from Jackie Chan, on par with others like Drunken Master and Fearless Hyena.

Little Mute is recommended into being able to take on the Shaolin Wooden Men, a tight spaced alley consisting of mechanical wooden dummies, attacking him from all directions. He has to defeat them all before the incense stick burns to the bottom, whilst his masters watch on. A really great scene here, showing Jackie's character going through the motions and hardship of lasting till the end. Once defeating them, Little

Mute is told to visit a place called evergreen and look someone will can help him, but trouble is only round the corner and little mute has to defend himself and others from a local gang. (One of them being the legendary Yuen Biao). During this time, the prisoner escapes after perfecting the Lions Roar technique and heads back to lead his feared Green Dragon Gang.

The Ex prisoner kills those responsible for putting him in chains, before heading back to the Shaolin Temple to take revenge. Chin Kang is awesome as the villain, taking on anyone with confidence and force. (He has a real screen presence)

Little Mute then returns to the Shaolin Temple and speaks to his master, who explains the prisoner was a former student who killed and then imprisoned for his actions. He gives little mute a book of secret instructions on the lost Shaolin techniques, in preparation for his upcoming fight with the ex prisoner. The training sequences here are fantastic, Jackie displaying awesome strength with handstand press-ups, having stone placed onto his back to further the punishment. The monks find out where the prisoner is hiding and ask little

mute to find him and bring him back. This leads to a great finale between Jackie and Chin Kang, With Little Mute learning the masked attacker was actually him. The finale gives us some great wide shots, allowing the audience to see the skill and timing involved into delivering a great fight scene for the fans.

Shaolin Wooden Men aka Shaolin Chamber Of Death, is one of Jackie's better Lo Wei movies. A movie which doesn't get spoken about a lot, a movie which I feel is a little under rated. Great fight scenes, great training sequences, great finale and plenty of shapes. The 88 Films release is fantastic, it really brings this movie alive from the older days of grainy vhs tapes and dodgy dvd releases.

Grab the movie if you haven't seen it, you won't be disappointed.

蛇形刁手 (1978)
Snake in the Eagle's Shadow
Box Office: HK $2,708,748.2

Snake In The Eagles Shadow is the movie that catapulted Jackie Chans career after being loaned out by Lo Wei to Seasonal Films. The movie was originally supposed to star Fu Sheng, but after Shaw Brothers placed such a large sum of get him, Director Yuen Woo Ping and Producer Ng See Yuen, went for Jackie Chan. They did have reservations at first with Jackie's previous movies under Lo Wei not doing so well at the box office. But both Yuen Woo Ping and Ng See Yuen knew Jackie could play this part well and the rest is history.

The movie open with leading villain ShangKuan (Hwang Jang Lee) challenging the leader of the Snake Fist School (Fung Hak On) after killing most of his students. ShangKuan says that he will kill all who have learnt the snake fist technique leading to a great fight between both men. ShangKuan is victorious and heads off to find Pai Chang Tien (Yuen Siu Tien), also known as the beggar.

Chien Fu (Jackie Chan) plays a servant in a Kung Fu school, mainly used by his elder as a punching bag to recruit new members. Chien isn't a fighter, but despite the beating, remains there in hope to one day learn. When out one day, Chien notices the old beggar in trouble and steps in to help fend off the attackers. A great scene where Chien thinks he's winning all on his own, only to be helped by the beggar all along. Chien offers him a place to stay and some food, which Pai Chang agrees too, but what Chien doesn't know is that Pai Chang is one of the last surviving Masters of the Snake Fist style. After Chien takes another beating from his elder just to gain some new members, Pai Chang decides he will teach this young man the first steps in Snake Fist Kung fu. He leaves Chien a message on the wall and foot prints on the floor to practise the movements. This is a classic scene, one I've watched time and time again over the years. Great musical score to build up the tension and seeing Chien improve and gain confidence is great to see, instead of having his confidence beat out of him.

Pai Chang is out knocking on doors begging for money when he quickly spots the snake sign pained on a wall. When he enters he is confronted by Su Chen (Hsu Hsia), who himself is also looking to kill Pai Chang. Great choreography in this short fight sequence, which ends with a priest (Roy Horan) entering the screen and both attacking Pai Chang (who escapes injured).

Back at the school of Chien Fu, his elder once again uses him as a punching bag for a fellow student to show what he's learnt to his father. Chien Fu has had enough beatings and finally decides to fight back, something Chien would regret after, taking another beating from his elder before running away. You can really feel the emotion by Chien Fu, sitting confused, beaten and very unhappy. Once again I have to mention the amazing musical score throughout this movie, it really does capture scenes like this perfectly.

Chien Fu and Pai Chang finally come back together, this time Chien looking after Pai Chang. Going back to his school undetected to bring medicine back, he nurses Pai Chang back to health. This is the first time we also get to see our three leading villains come together, ShangKuan, The Priest and Su Chien. Plotting to kill Pai Chang, a forth person comes into play, wearing a mask and sharing information about his whereabouts.

The training sequences in this movie are amazing, Pai Chang finally agrees to teach Chien Fu Snake Fist, first learning the stances, followed by Strength and conditioning his wrists for attacks and defence. The famous grabbing the eggs scene was also used for the Tekken game based on Jackie's character, showing it's cultural impact many years after.

Back at the school, a challenge comes to fight the best student and easily defeats him, at this time the master comes back home, much to Chiens delight. Chien steps in and showcases his snake fist to the amazement of the other students. Watching in the shadows is ShangKuan, who realises Chien must know where Pai Chang is and cons him into believing he's an old friend after beating Chien in a fight using the snake style. This is where we get to see Hwang Jang Lee showing his amazing kicking skills, speed and power.

Afterwards Chien is at home and witnesses a cat being attacked by a snake and the

cat defending itself with its claws. This is when Chien realises he can combine both the snake and cat together to make his own style. Su Chien attacks Pai Chang, bad idea, Pai Chang quickly dispatches of Sun Chien and heads back to Chien Fu. The cook who works at the school, poisons the tea, not realising they already know he's the one giving there whereabouts away and switched the tea. Chien Fu then faces off against the priest, the priest played by Roy Horan could only use one arm due to injuring his other. The sword is used in this scene would actually connect and slash Jackie's arm and left him in pain whilst the cameras still rolled.

The finale between Jackie Chan and Hwang Jang Lee is worth the money alone. The scene where Hwang Jang Lee delivers a flying kick to Jackie's face, actually knocked Jackie's front tooth out his mouth. You can see in the fight Jackie's gap in his teeth, back then they didn't have CGI or time to for a new tooth, just keep rolling and finish the scene.

I love this movie, the friendship between Chien Fu and Pai Chang, the training sequences, great fights and an awesome music score. Snake in the Eagles Shadow is a classic and one for any fan to see, buy and watch again. Hwang Jang Lee is once again in fine kicking form, Yuen Woo Ping and his team delivering a great movie and one that would change Jackie Chan's career forever. Remember, "The Snake Bites". A must see.

JACKIE CHAN CAMEO STORY

HIS TOP 10 HK CINEMA CAMEOS
By Paul Bramhall

Over the last few years many of Jackie Chan's classics from the 70's, 80's and 90's have found a new audience thanks to the stellar work of labels like 88 Films, Arrow Video, and Eureka! Entertainment. Arguably one of the most physically talented performers of the last 50 years, Chan was for many the ultimate action star – combining martial arts prowess, a willingness to put his body on the line for increasingly daring stunts, and that all important screen presence that kept audiences glued to the screen.

Understandably Chan become a much sought-after commodity, and his presence (or even just involvement) in a production became a way to increase a movies box office appeal. As a result the star has made cameo appearances in a number of productions over the years, ranging from simply lending his presence by appearing in a single scene, to also being involved behind the scenes by assisting to choreograph the action.

In this feature we chronologically count down 10 of his cameo appearances in Hong Kong productions (and 2 outliers just for the fun of it), which will hopefully attract audiences just becoming familiar with Chan's output to some of Hong Kong cinemas wider offerings!

Pom Pom (1984) – The first in a series of comedic outings that feature a pair of loser cops played by Richard Ng and John Shum, the 4 Pom Pom movies ran concurrently with Sammo Hung's Lucky Stars series, and it could well be argued that Pom Pom wouldn't exist without the previous years Winners and Sinners (which also starred Ng and Shum). Taking a similar approach to slapstick comedic shenanigans, only without the action scenes that Sammo Hung's Lucky Stars franchise would be

imbued with, most likely due to Hung's role as producer here we also get Jackie Chan in a blink and you'll miss it cameo. Playing a motorbike riding traffic cop, ironically 4 years later we'd see Chan in a similar role at the start of Police Story II.

Naughty Boys (1986) – Director Wellson Chin's comedy Naughty Boys offers up another blink and you'll miss it cameo from Chan, however this time he was much more involved behind the scenes (even having his face appear on the poster!). Both Chan and his Stuntmen Association were responsible for the action in this comedy about a group of diamond thieves, one

which offers up a rare starring role for fellow Jackie Chan Stuntmen Association member Mars, paired up with leading ladies Kara Hui and Carina Lau. Apart from being able to glimpse Chan choreographing some of the finale's action in the behind-the-scenes footage that plays over the end credits, he can also be spotted in the movie itself playing an inmate in a prison scene.

A Kid from Tibet (1992) – By the 1990's both Jackie Chan and Sammo Hung had several directorial credits to their names, but for the youngest of the 3 Dragons, Yuen Biao, it would take until 1992 for him to make his directorial debut (and so far only time in the director's chair) with A Kid from Tibet. Like his Peking Opera brothers Biao also uses his debut as a starring vehicle for himself, playing a Tibetan monk who travels to Hong Kong in pursuit of a powerful treasure that's been stolen. Perhaps as a

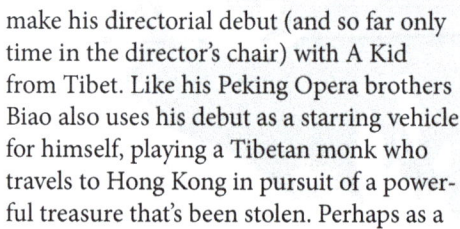

show of support, upon Biao's monks' arrival in Hong Kong airport, while disembarking he bumps into another passenger going in the other direction, played by Jackie Chan. Interestingly, the scene was re-created in 2005's Tom Yum Goong, with Tony Jaa bumping into a Jackie Chan lookalike!

Project S (1993) – Perhaps the most infamous of all Chan's cameo's, Project S was a spin-off from Police Story 3: Supercop (even being called Supercop 2 in some territories), offering up a leading role for Michelle Yeoh as the Mainland cop who's partnered with Chan in the 3rd Police Story entry. In what very much feels like a standalone scene, Chan shows up as Chan Ka Kui disguised in drag, involving a wig and figure-hugging red dress, in an attempt to foil a jewellery store robbery by Eric Tsang (who is also in drag and clocking in a cameo appearance!). Chan's appearance

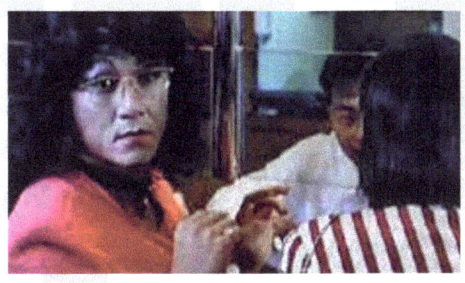

here feels more like an excuse for distributors to put his face on the poster in some countries, however it at least offers up a brief dose of his distinct style of action before the rest of the movie is handed over to Yeoh.

King of Comedy (1999) – In 1999 Hong Kong comedy legend Stephen Chow and Jackie Chan agreed to clock in cameo appearances in each other's productions. Chow showed up as a cop in Chan's Gorgeous (in what's arguably the funniest scene in the entire movie, and ridiculously one which was cut from the US release!), and

in King of Comedy Chan shows up as a stuntman working on a movie that Chow's character is playing an extra in. The story of an unknown actor trying to make it in the industry, King of Comedy offers up an equal amount of both drama and comedic beats, and seeing Chan essentially playing a version of himself on-set (in a scene clearly paying homage to the finale of John Woo's The Killer) makes for one of his best cameo appearances.

Gen-X Cops (1999) – On the brink of the new millennium it seemed like Chan was keen to ensure the Hong Kong action genre was left in good hands (presumably while he continued to cash cheques in Hollywood), and the result was Gen-X Cops. Featuring a line-up of the most popular young stars of the era (re: most of the Young and Dangerous cast), Chan was onboard as executive producer, and also brought in several members of his stunt team (including Nicky Li as action choreographer) to lend their action credentials. Chan's involvement technically already

allowed distributors to preface the title with 'Jackie Chan Presents', but perhaps as a safety net to ensure audiences didn't feel too duped, he also clocked in a brief comedy relief cameo as a fisherman.

Enter the Phoenix (2003) – After spending most of the new millennium in Hollywood, Chan would return to Hong Kong in 2004 to headline New Police Story, but before doing so he'd warm up audiences in 2003 with a couple of cameos, the first of which

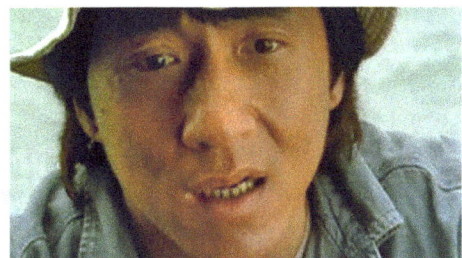

would be in Stephen Fung's directorial debut Enter the Phoenix. Co-produced by Chan's JCE Movies Limited, the comedic plot revolves around the mistaken identity of the gay successor to Yuen Biao's triad boss, and Chan clocks in a brief final scene cameo. On a sidenote, this would be the first time for Chan and Yuen Biao to appear in a movie together since A Kid from Tibet, although they never appear onscreen together (for that audiences would need to wait another 3 years for 2006's Rob-B-Hood).

The Twins Effect (2003) – Intended as a starring vehicle for Hong Kong pop duo Twins, for The Twins Effect director Dante Lam called up Chan to clock in a "Special Friendly Appearance" (that's what its listed as in the credits!) to help bolster proceedings. Naturally, his character's name is Jackie. Chan's cameo consists of a couple of scenes, one where he weds Karen Mok, and the other more significant one has him driving an ambulance while fending off motorbike riding gweilo vampires. Although the action direction is credited to Donnie Yen, his inevitable scuffle with the vampires feels distinctly Chan-esque,

offering up a lite version of his trademark comedic style imbued with several wire-work infused moments. Surprisingly, Ekin Chen's fight scene is far more entertaining, not something I ever thought I'd write.

The Twins Effect II (2004) – After the success of the previous years The Twins Effect, a sequel was inevitably released the following year. Completely unconnected to its predecessor in every way, here we get a clunky fantasy involving a world where men have become enslaved to women, one which features the debut of Chan's son – Jaycee Chan. Once more, Chan here is brought in to bust out some action, this time as an ancient warrior who's been encased for centuries as a terracotta warrior. It's Donnie Yen that wakes him up, providing a re-match from their face

off in Shanghai Knights the year prior, as the pair swirl around in a deluge of early 2000's CGI projectiles, water works, and slow motion. Is it possible for 2 movies to waste the talents of having Chan and Yen share the screen together in as many years? Apparently yes.

All U Need is Love (2021) – Coming almost 10 years since Chan last appeared in a Hong Kong production, in 2021 director Vincent Kok (who previously worked with Chan on 1999's Gorgeous) brought him on-

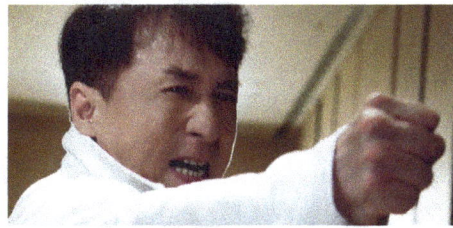

board to cameo in the charity production All U Need is Love, made to raise funds for out-of-work members of the Hong Kong filmmaking community due to the Covid-19 pandemic. Taking place in a locked down hotel due to a sudden outbreak of the virus, Chan's appearance as a member of the Pandemic Task Force essentially amounts to him punching Ken Lo set to the Police Story theme, and little else. However just to see Chan appear in a Hong Kong production in 2021, despite him falling out of favour with local audiences a long time ago, brings an undeniable feeling of nostalgia.

Fearless Hyena II (1983) – Forever likely to be known as the production that Chan walked away from in the early stages having had a bust up with producer Lo Wei, far from abandoning ship, Wei decided to plough on and use any means necessary to put out a finished product. Said finished product involved incorporating unused scenes from the original Fearless Hyena, recycling footage from both Fearless Hyena (including the finale!) and Spiritual Kung Fu, and placing a fake beard on a completely unconvincing Chan double to film any scenes needed to glue the story together. The end result is an incoherent mess, and one which contains so little new footage of Chan in action that, despite star billing, his role can essentially be described as barely more than a cameo in his own movie.

The Founding of a Republic (2009) – A whole 5 years before Xi Jinping urged the local film industry to make "patriotism the main theme of literary and artistic creation", kicking off a wave of Mainland Melody movies that continues to this day, 2009's The Founding of a Republic was somewhat ahead the curve. Made as part of the PRC's 60th anniversary celebrations and partly funded by the government, the almost 140-minute epic details the rousing tale of Mao Zedong's rise to power between 1945 and 1949. Released at a time when Hong Kong actors were still a box office draw in the Mainland, directors Huang Jianxin and Han Sanping populated the runtime with cameos from the likes of Andy Lau, Donnie Yen, Jet Li, and – you guessed it – Jackie Chan also briefly turns up playing a Hong Kong journalist.

Added note from Editor

The Black Tavern (1972)
I recently was reminded that Jackie had multiple roles as a cameo in Another Shaw production with an early appearance fighting next to Mars who would later become an important member of the Jackie Chan Stunt Team. This movie appearance of Jackie's is not very well known and you have to freeze frame to confirm it's him but he does appear in several scenes the final one being speared by a sword

The Golden Lotus (1974) Jackie makes several appearances Brother Yun [Pear seller] a movie that will only be watched by Shaw brother fans and Jackie Chan completest

The Scottish Connection

Exploring Mary McGoldrick's Passion for
JACKIE CHAN
Memorabilia

In the world of dedicated collectors, few can match the enthusiasm and devotion of Mary Margaret McGoldrick. A proud resident of Scotland, Mary has spent countless years building an awe-inspiring collection of Jackie Chan memorabilia. As a true Jackie Chan super fan, she has amassed a vast assortment of items that pay tribute to the legendary martial artist and actor. Today, we have the privilege of delving into Mary's treasure trove, as she graciously grants us a sneak peek at some of her most beloved possessions.

Mary's journey as a Jackie Chan aficionado began many years ago, sparked by her admiration for his unparalleled talent and unique style. Over time, her passion evolved into an all-consuming endeavour to acquire as many pieces of Chan-related memorabilia as possible. From rare movie posters to autographed photographs, figurines, and even clothing worn by the star himself, Mary's collection knows no bounds.

One glance at Mary's collection is enough to leave anyone in awe. Among her prized possessions is an original movie poster from Jackie Chan's breakout film "Drunken Master," which is widely regarded as a martial arts classic. The poster, adorned with vibrant colours and showcasing Chan's signature moves, serves as a testament to his iconic status in the world of cinema.

Another remarkable item in Mary's collection is a set of autographed photographs that capture personal moments from Chan's illustrious career. These snapshots not only exhibit the star's charm and charisma but also offer a glimpse into the behind-the-scenes world of filmmaking. Mary cherishes these mementos as cherished glimpses into the life of her idol.

Mary's collection also extends beyond paper and photographs. She proudly displays an assortment of intricately crafted figurines, each one meticulously capturing the essence of Jackie Chan's on-screen personas. From his comedic antics to his gravity-defying stunts, these figurines serve as three-dimensional embodiments of the actor's unparalleled talent and charisma.

As impressive as Mary's collection already is, it shows no signs of stopping. With an unwavering dedication to her favorite actor, she continues to hunt down new additions, seeking out rare and unique pieces that will further enhance her collection. It is not an exaggeration to say that Mary's collection could very well become one of the most extensive Jackie Chan memorabilia compilations in all of Scotland.

We extend our sincerest gratitude to Mary Margaret McGoldrick for granting us this exclusive opportunity to glimpse her extraordinary collection. Her unwavering passion for Jackie Chan's work and her dedication to preserving his legacy through her collection is truly remarkable. Mary's story serves as a reminder of the profound impact that beloved artists can have on our lives and the ways in which their influence can inspire us to pursue our passions with unwavering determination.

In conclusion, Mary Margaret McGoldrick's collection of Jackie Chan memorabilia stands as a testament to the power of fandom and the enduring appeal of one of the world's greatest action stars. Her unwavering dedication and passion have transformed her collection into a remarkable archive, a true testament to the indelible mark left by Jackie Chan's cinematic legacy. As Mary continues her quest to expand her collection, we can only imagine the extraordinary treasures that await her in the future.

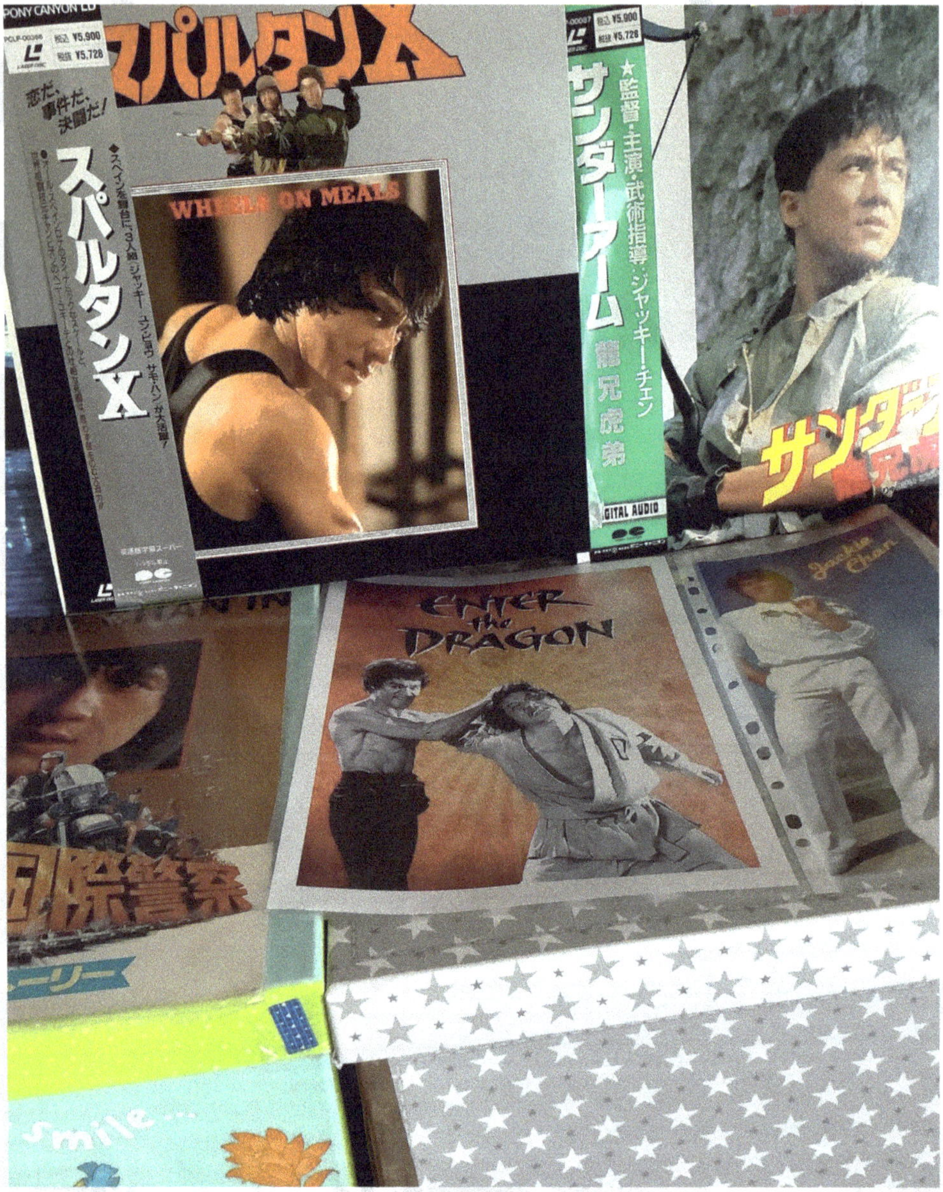
PONY CANYON LD
スパルタンX
WHEELS ON MEALS
サンダーアーム
龍兄虎弟
DIGITAL AUDIO
ENTER the DRAGON

PROTECTOR
RUSH HOUR

AMEX PHOTO GALLERY
KUNG FU? JC & CARRADINE
DRAGONS FOREVER
OPERATION CONDOR
POLICE STORY 2
SCREEN POWER
THE JACKIE CHAN MAGAZINE
EXCLUSIVE!!! JACKIE IN LONDON
CHARITY SOFTBALL
JACKIE CHAN

DRUNK MONKEY
JACKIE CHAN
SHAOLIN WOODEN MEN

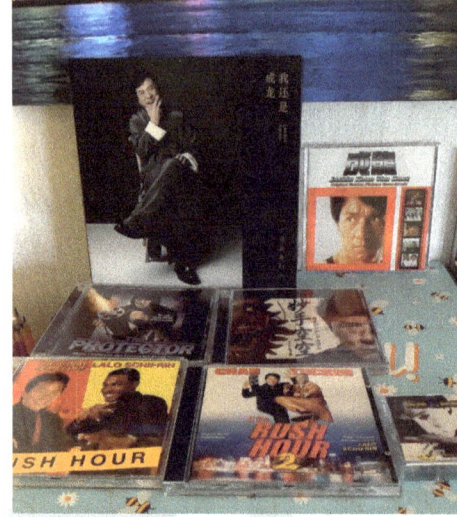

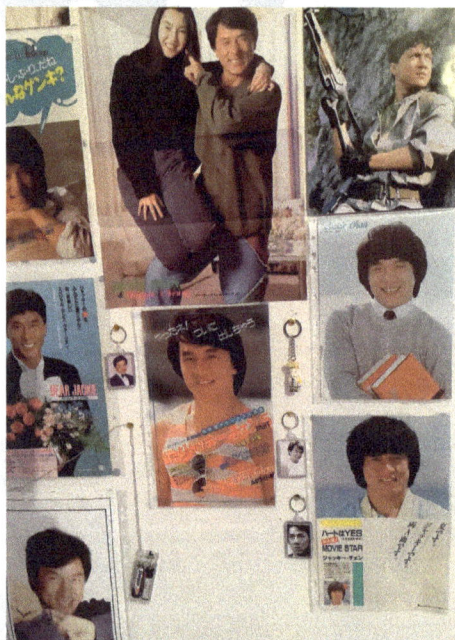

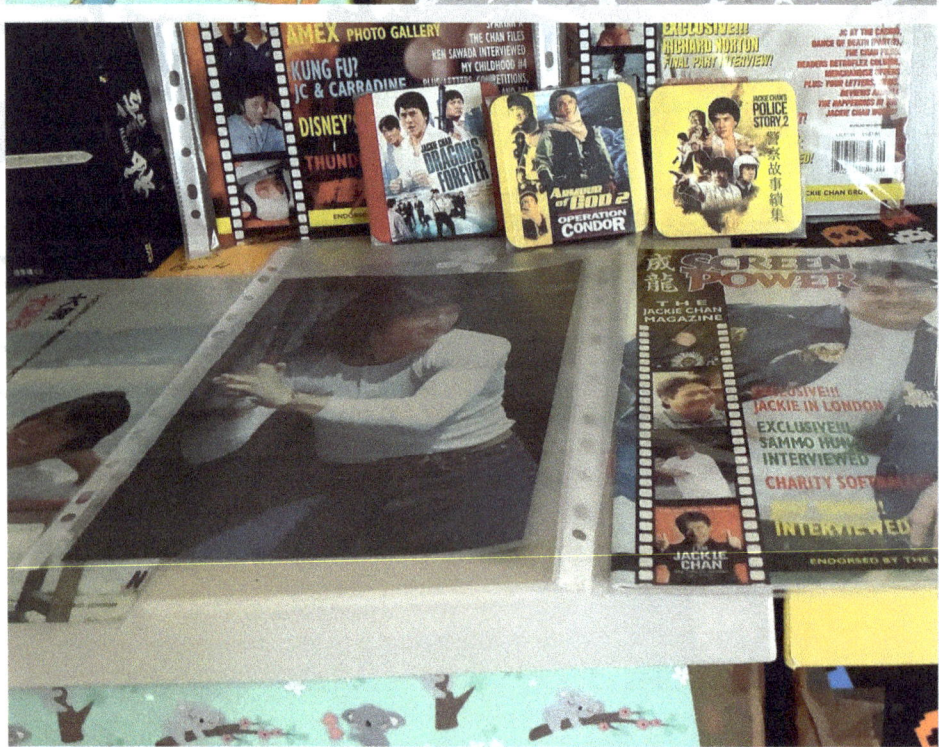

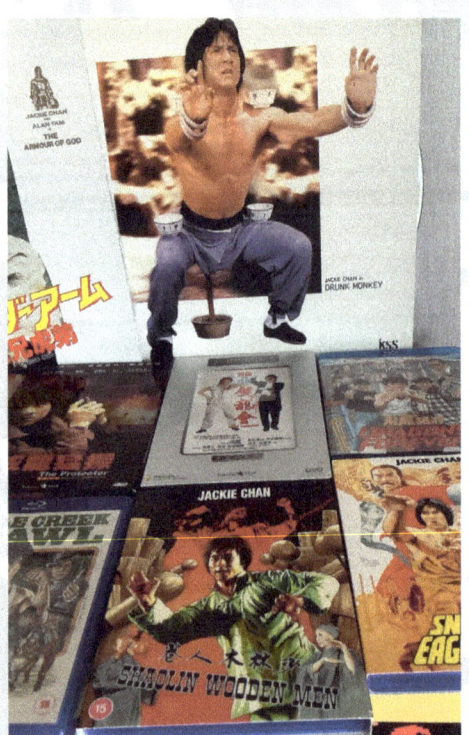

PlayStation 2
ACKIE CHAN
TWIN DRAGONS
DRAGON LORD

ELMER

PAINTED FACES
PAINTED FACES
PAINTED FACES
PAINTED FACES
PAINTED FACES
PAINTED FACES

THE POLICE STORY
THE POLICE STORY

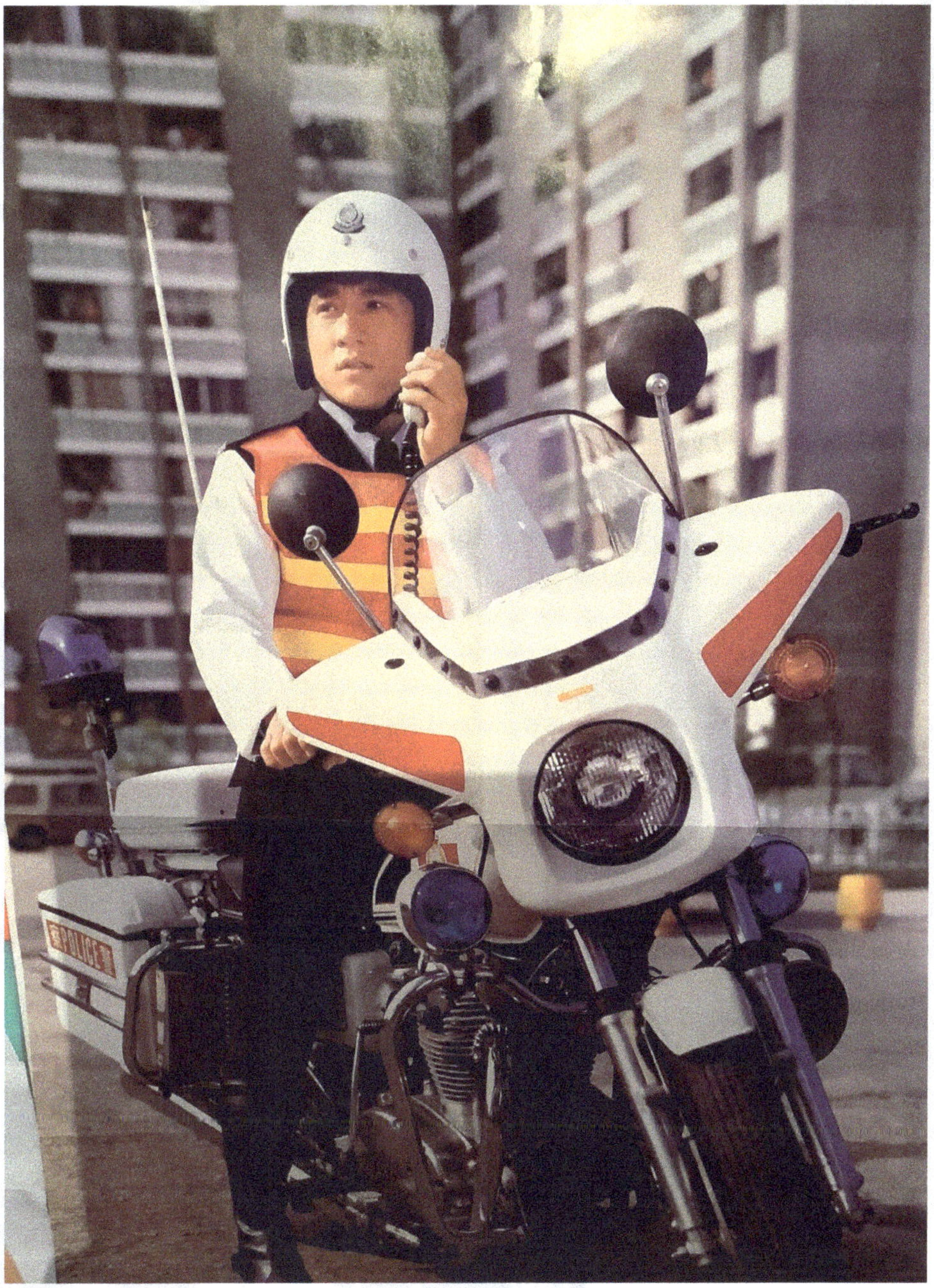

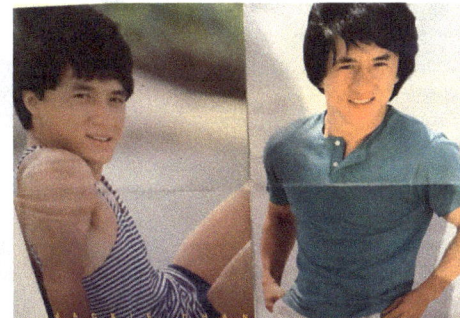

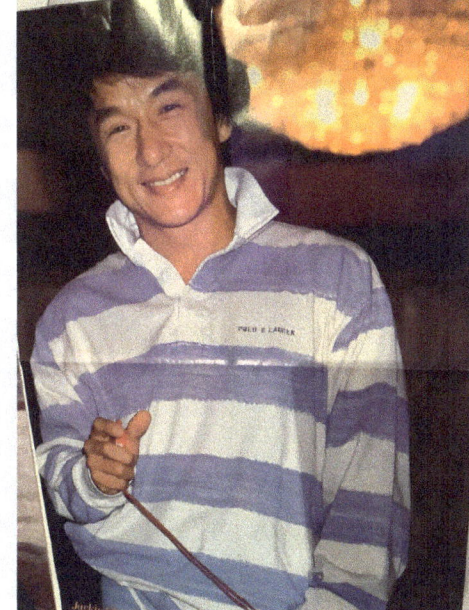

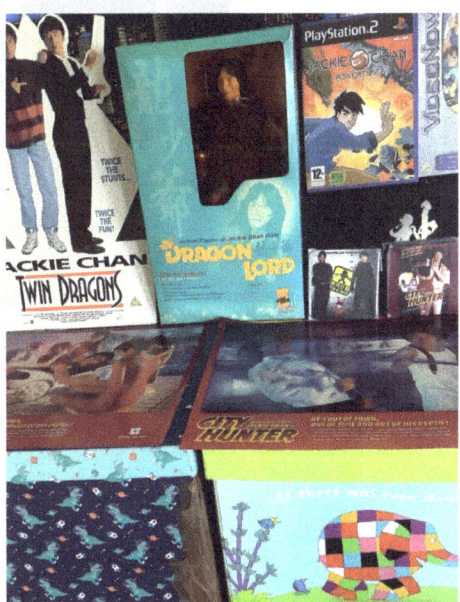

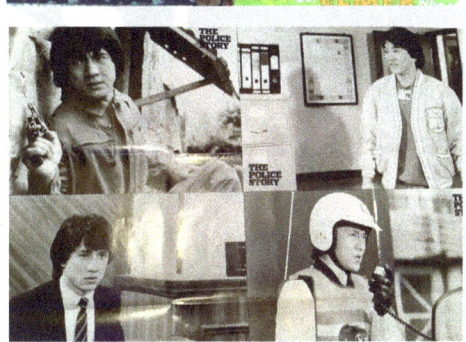

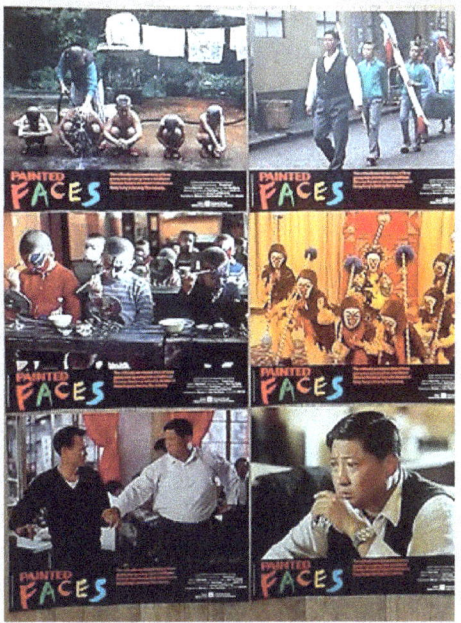

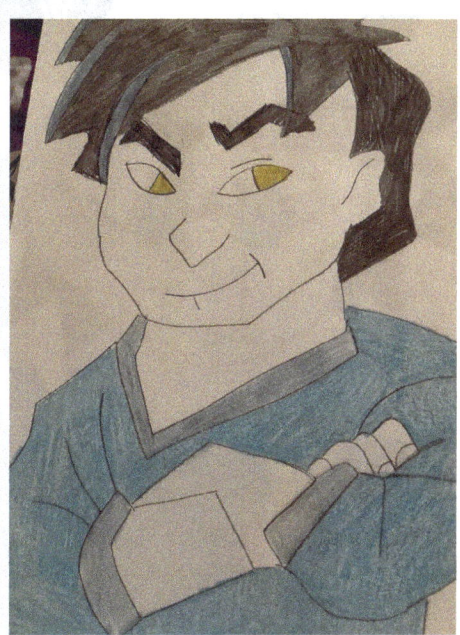

SELECTED LOBBY CARD GALLLERY

成龍

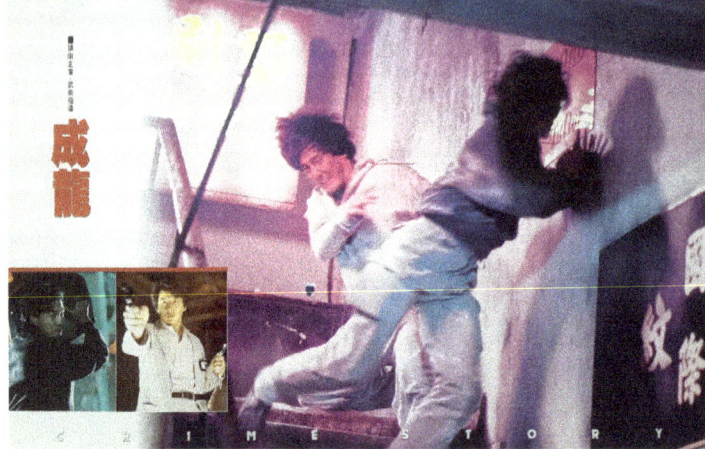

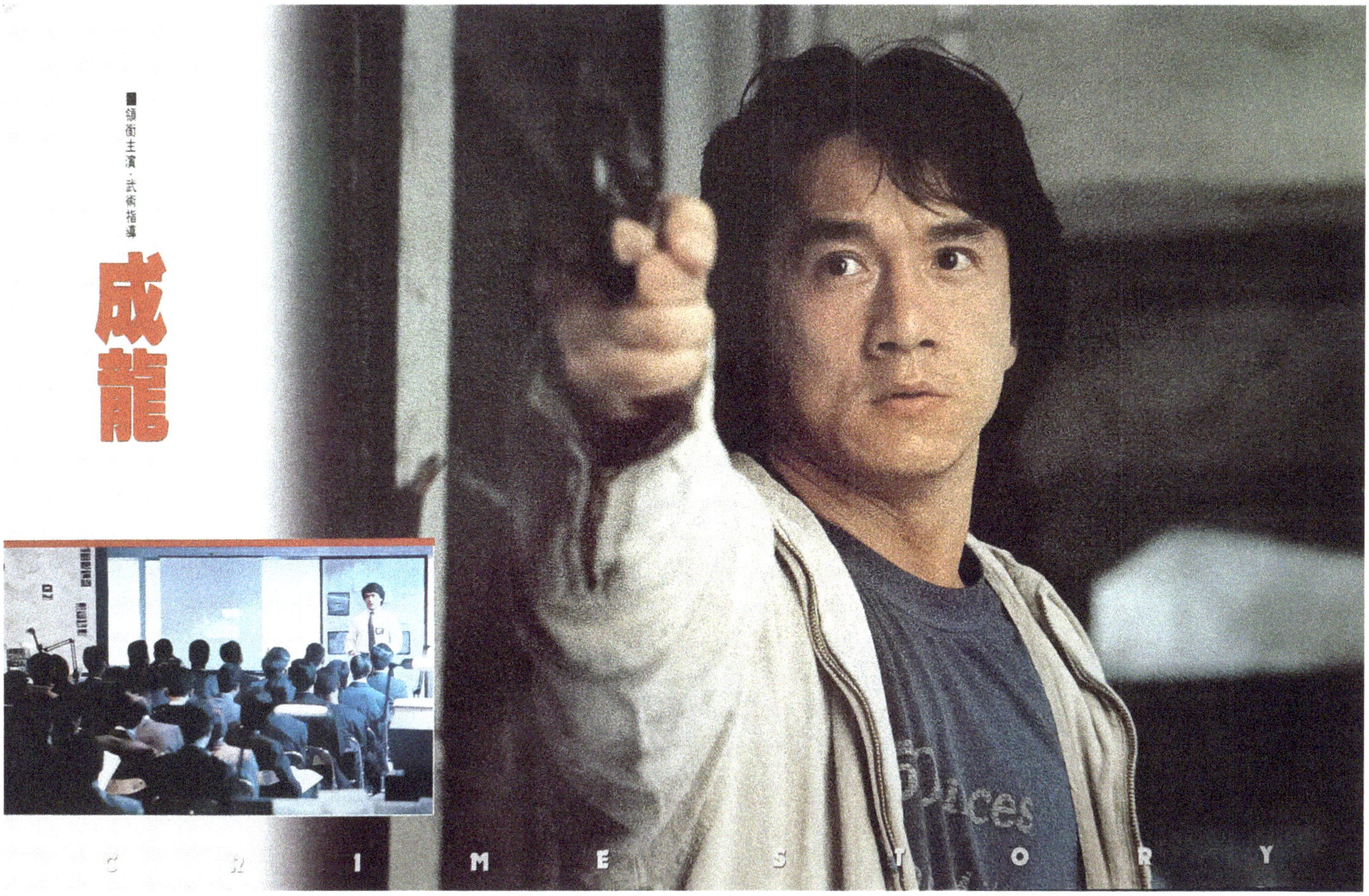
■領銜主演・武術指導
成龍
C R I M E S T O R Y

成龍
黃志強
陳誌華
何冠昌
蔡瀾
C R I M E S T O R Y

重案組
C R I M E S T O R Y

黎傑 鍾勉強
羅秀慧 胡素玲
周震東 詹偉偉 劉嘉蔚 朱偉光
秦天南 張志成 陳德森
張丁平 雷楚雄 陸子峯
張耀宗
劉俊強 林國華 潘恒生 黃岳泰 陳廣鴻
莊志真 張學潤
黃霑
李宗盛
C R I M E S T O R Y

成龍
黃志強
陳誌華
成龍 成家班
尹發 鍾發 段偉倫 尹相林 夏占士
朱國樑 陳德光 田哲文
C R I M E • S T O R Y

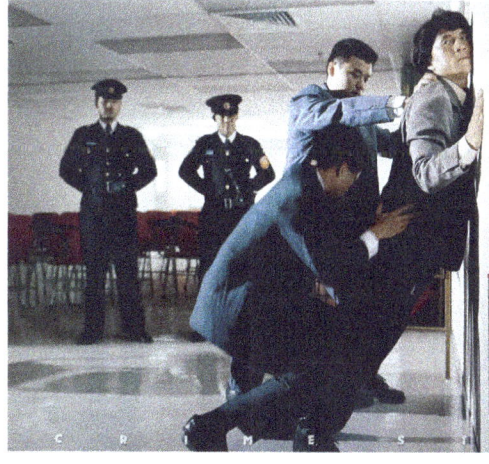

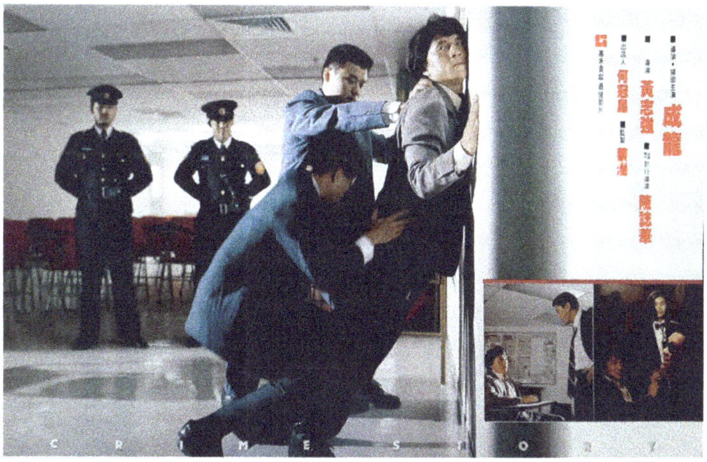

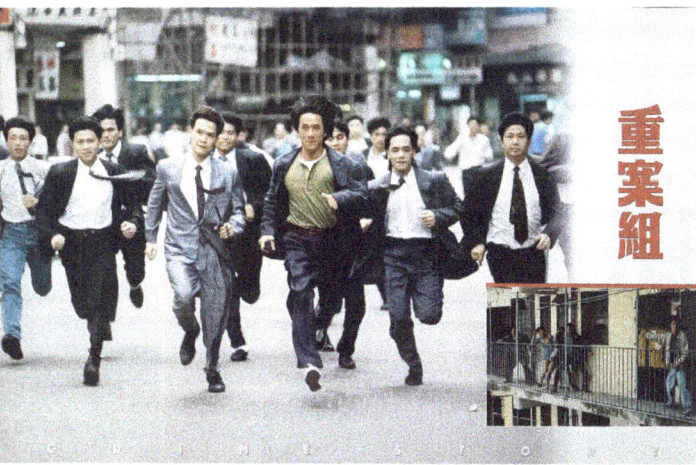

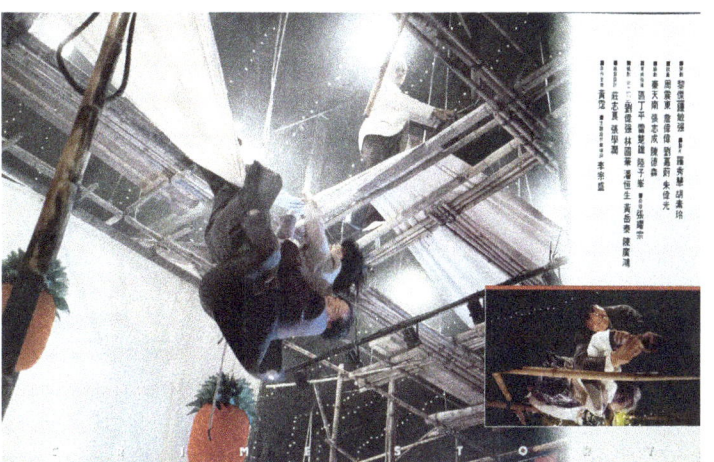

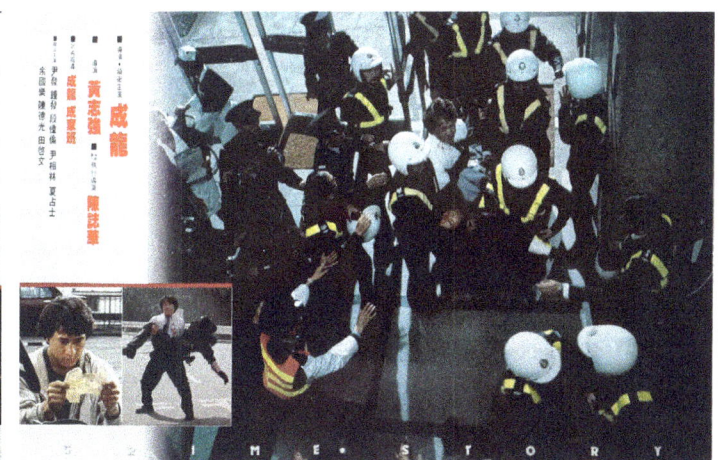

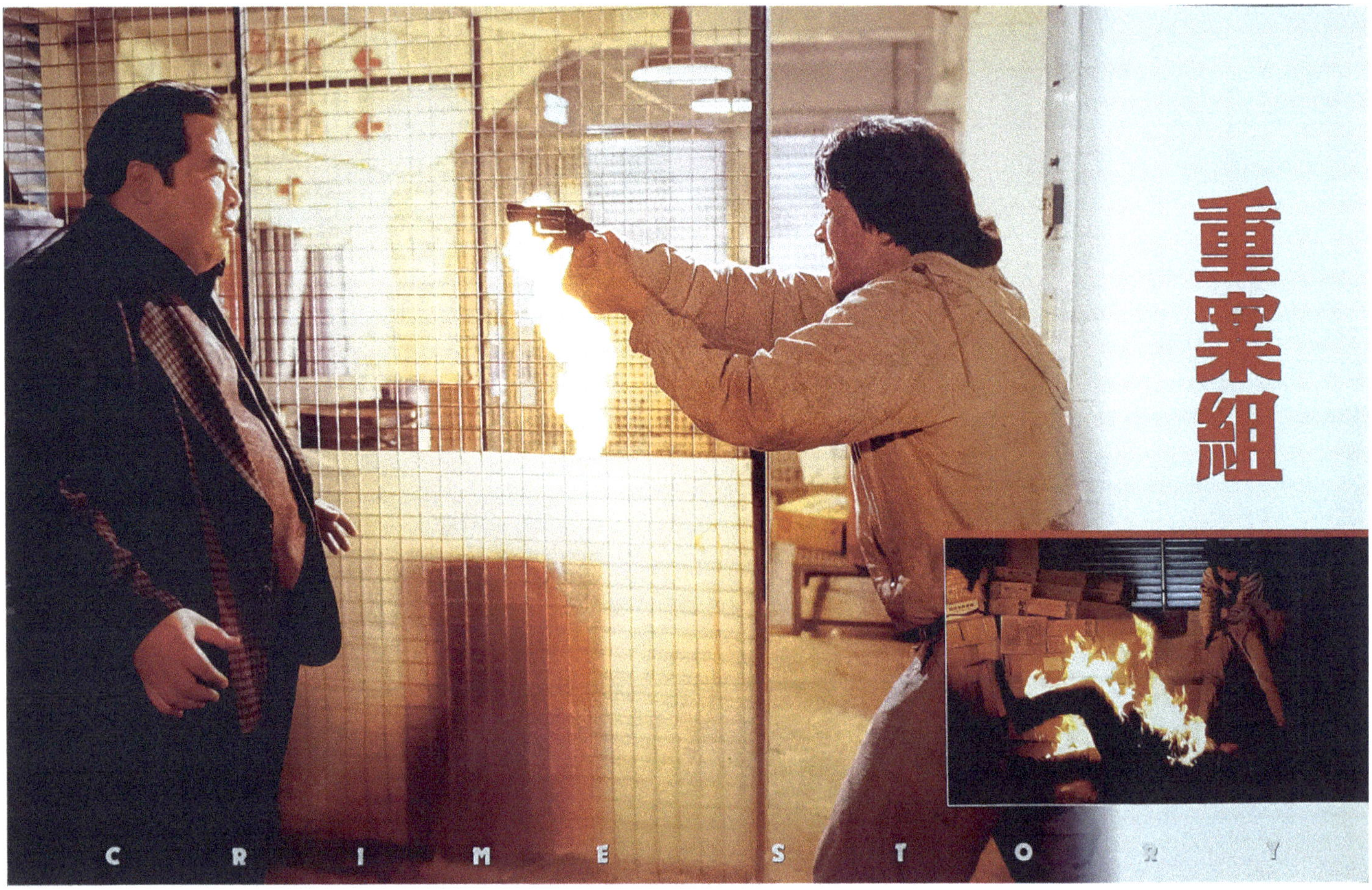
重案組
C R I M E S T O R Y

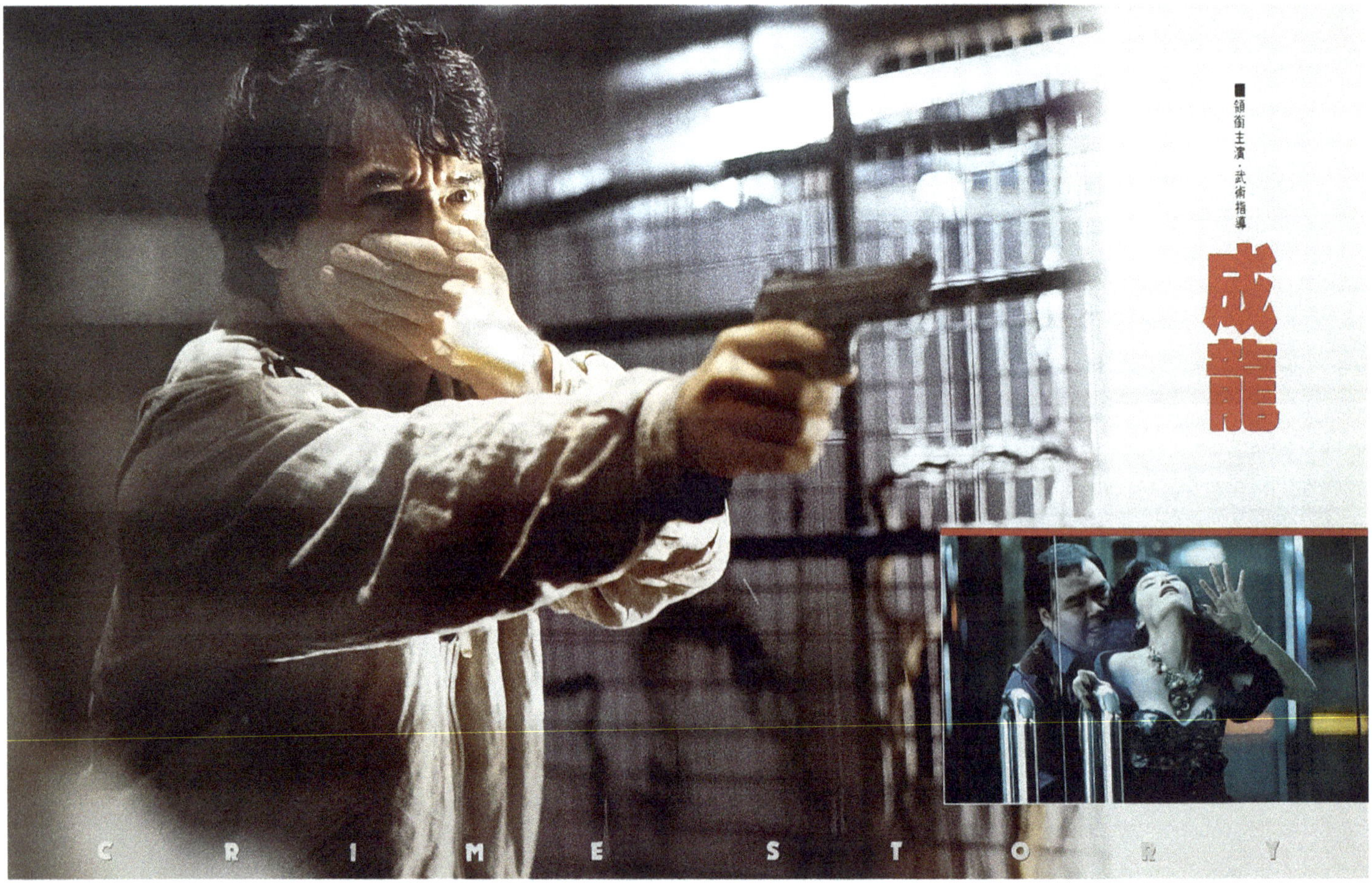
■領銜主演·武術指導
成龍
C R I M E S T O R Y

重案組

CRIME STORY

■導演・領銜主演 **成龍**
■導演 **黃志強** ■執行導演 **陳詠華**
■出品人 **何冠昌** ■監製 **蔡瀾**
■嘉禾貢獻最佳影片

CRIME STORY

Custom Lobby cards by the
Jackie Chan Appreciation Group

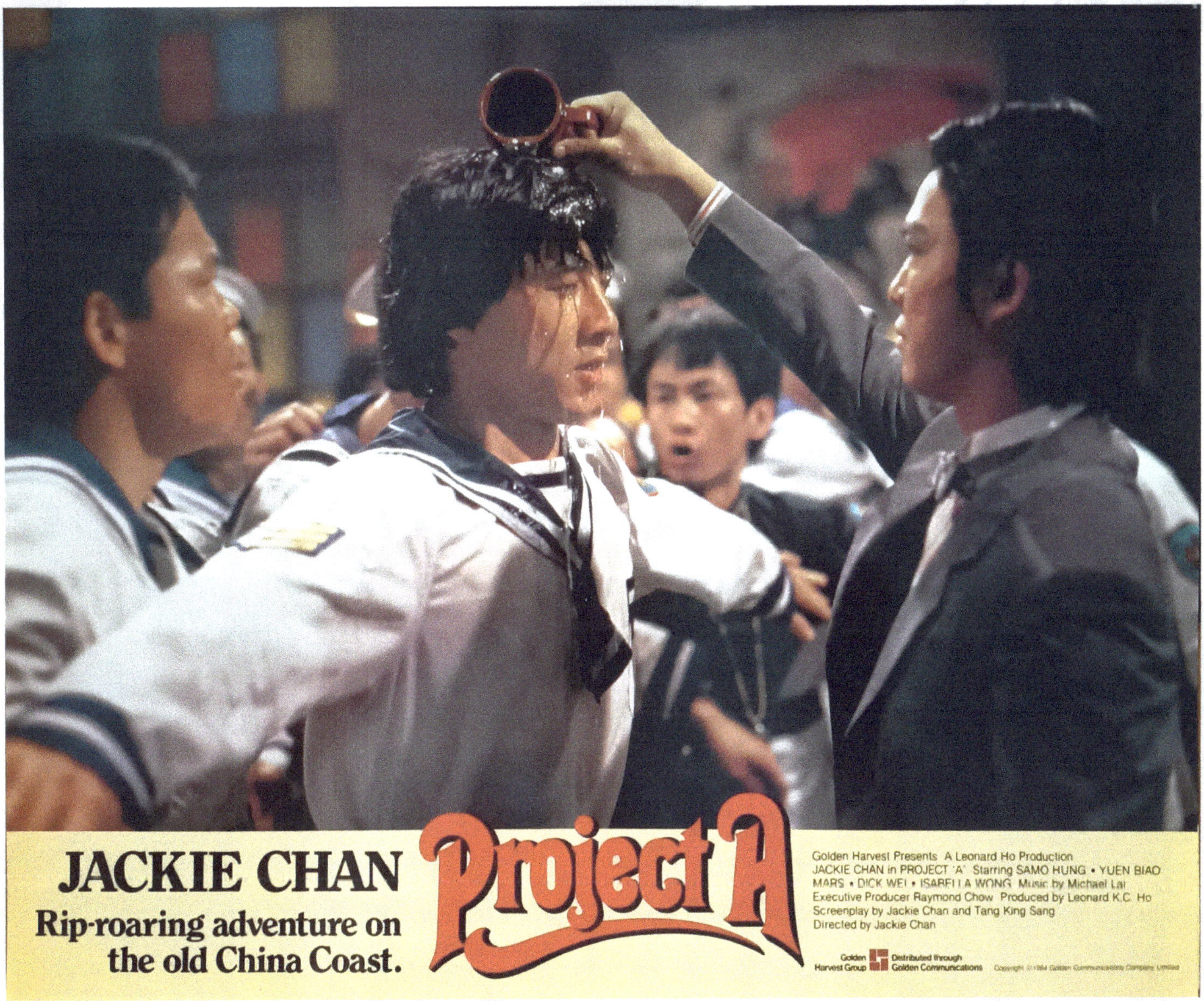
JACKIE CHAN
Rip-roaring adventure on the old China Coast.
Project A
Golden Harvest Presents A Leonard Ho Production
JACKIE CHAN in PROJECT 'A' Starring SAMO HUNG • YUEN BIAO
MARS • DICK WEI • ISABELLA WONG Music by Michael Lai
Executive Producer Raymond Chow Produced by Leonard K.C. Ho
Screenplay by Jackie Chan and Tang King Sang
Directed by Jackie Chan
Golden Harvest Group
Distributed through Golden Communications

JACKIE CHAN
Rip-roaring adventure on the old China Coast.
Project A

JACKIE CHAN
Rip-roaring adventure on the old China Coast.
Project A

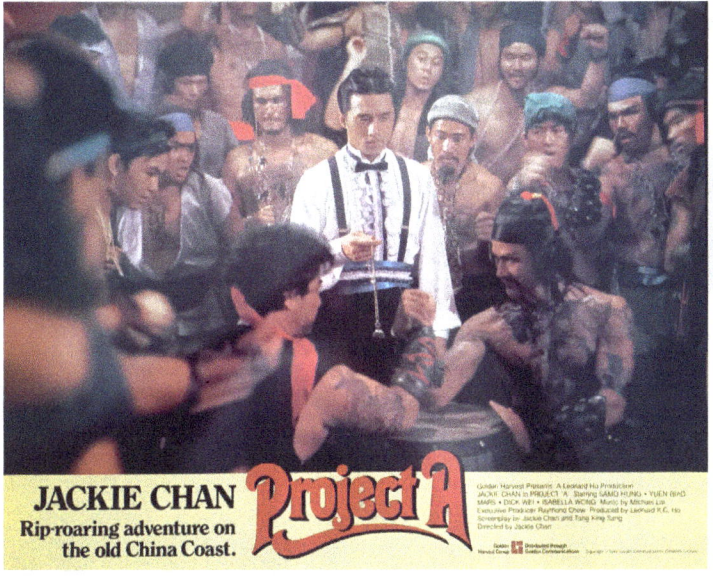

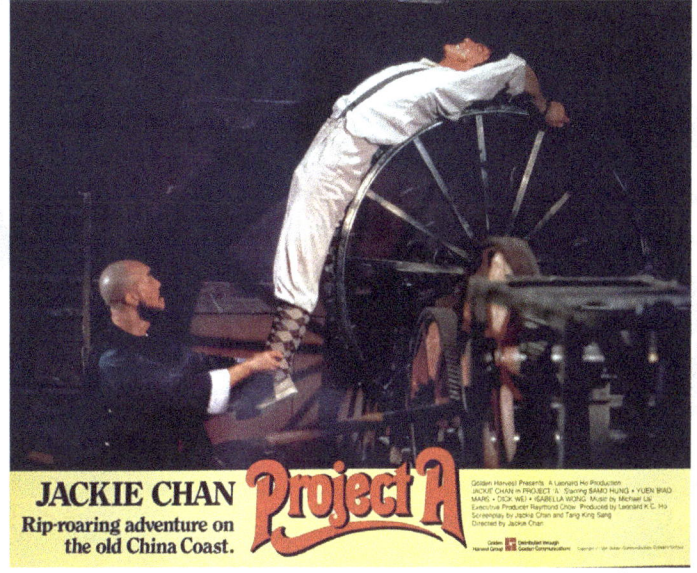

THANK YOU'S

Special Thanks to

Darren Wheeling (cover Art) USA
Tim Hollingsworth Design and interior layout
Paul Bramhall (Contributer) Australia
Mike Nesbitt (contributor) UK
Thorsten Boose (Contributor) Germany
Simon Pritchard (Contributor/ Staff)
Johnny Burnett (contributor) Scotland
Mary Margaret McGoldrick (Collector) Scotland

Without you this magazine would not happen

Rick Baker Editor/Publisher
All articles Copyright Eastern Heroes

www.ingramcontent.com/pod-product-compliance
Lightning Source LLC
Chambersburg PA
CBHW061124170426

43209CB00013B/1666

www.ingramcontent.com/pod-product-compliance
Lightning Source LLC
Chambersburg PA
CBHW061124170426
43209CB00013B/1665